First Edition

Chris Lopez & Jason Wells

www.AntiSuitEntrepreneur.com

Anti Suit Entrepreneur: Live Life On Your Terms, Escape The Suit & Tie and Learn New Rules for the Economy by Chris Lopez and Jason Wells

Anti Suit Entrepreneur Books
316 California Ave #767
Reno, NV 89509
775-298-5121
http://www.AntiSuitEntrepreneur.com

Cover Design: Jason Wells, Anti Suit Entrepreneur Books
Library of Congress Control Number: 2013953172
ISBN-10: 0989648303
ISBN-13: 978-0989648301

For general information on our other products and services or for technical support please contact Anti Suit Entrepreneur Company at 775-298-5121 or http://www.AntiSuitEntrepreneur.com

Contents

Chapter 1

Live Life on Your Terms

"I want to drive off the bridge," Chris thought to himself while sitting in Washington D.C. commuter traffic. While sitting in bumper to bumper traffic inhaling exhaust fumes, his mind wandered off into a hazy daydream about what his life would be like if he kept on his current path. None of the outcomes were appealing. In fact, some even made him shudder with despair. The traffic finally inching forward snapped him back to reality.

"I can't imagine doing this for the next 30 years of my life." Chris promised himself that his life would not just consist of commuting hours a day to a job he was so-so about. "There has to be more to life!"

Jason, in his seventh year of running his family's law firm, sat at his desk pondering his future. He was about to graduate law school, become a lawyer, and deal with both running the law firm and taking cases to court. He started agonizing over what the rest of his life would be like. Every week would consist of fighting insurance adjustors, arguing with attorneys, tackling mountains of paperwork, and getting up early (which he dreaded) so he could look forward to kissing judges' asses, all while wearing a suit and tie, which would feel like a noose around his neck. He thought to himself, "What the hell am I doing?" How many times have you had thoughts like that? Probably more than you care to count. Everyone has, including us.

However, we both hit our boiling points in 2002 and escaped a life of mediocrity by becoming Anti Suit Entrepreneurs. This book is our story about how we escaped the suit and tie, learned the new rules of the economy, and now live life on our terms, and how you can, too.

Victim of First World Problems

Chances are you are reading this book because you are not completely satisfied with your current life and work situation. Maybe, like us, you hate commuting and wearing a suit and tie to a job that just pays the bills. Perhaps the repetitive monotony of your work is slowly driving you insane.

Or the thought of doing your dead-end job is like dragging finger nails across a chalkboard. Maybe you just had bad timing when you were born and are now trying to start your career at a bad time in the economy and not much is available. There are hundreds of different variations that we could cover. Regardless of whether or not we stated your situation, you know what it is.

Your situation is not great, but it is not that horrible either when you put it into perspective. Compared to most people living in third world countries, you have it great! You have clean drinking water whenever you want, food to eat, and a roof over your head. Your basic survival needs are not only met, but surpassed, big time.

So, you should be completely happy and content, right? Wrong.

As we like to say, "You're a victim of first world problems." You are fortunate enough to live in a first world country where all your basic survival needs are met, yet you are not content and want more from life. Since you are not worrying about where your next meal is coming from, there is no urgency or underlying survival need to improve your situation immediately. Your situation just continues to drag on, day by day, stuck in mediocrity.

Life of Mediocrity

Years ago we identified *living a life of mediocrity* as enemy #1; since we live in a first world country, mediocrity often settles in our lives without us being aware of it. A life of mediocrity is just going through the motions, working jobs that you do not love or that do not have the desired impact on society. This mediocrity can lead to not doing or achieving what you want in life because you lack the time or money. All the while years fly by and before you know it, your dream list of to-do's has turned into a regret list full of "woulda, coulda, and shoulda's."

That's enemy #1. Unfortunately, it is just too damn easy to fall into a life of unchanging mediocrity, because it is easy to fill your life with busy work, excuses, and procrastination. Mediocrity slowly creeps into your life.

Probably reading about mediocrity is stirring up some thoughts and emotions for you. And they are probably uncomfortable. Very uncomfortable. No one likes thinking about his own excuses and reasons for staying in mediocrity because it opens a can of worms into all sorts of self issues and "skeletons in the closet." But facing those issues is exactly what needs to be done in order to escape mediocrity.

That's what the Anti Suit Entrepreneur is all about: escaping mediocrity.

The Anti Suit Entrepreneur

As people see the way we have complete control over our schedules, freedom to do what we want, and the money to do so, they inevitably ask, "So... how are you able to that?" That question has been asked to us thousands of times because people are intrigued by what we do and how we are able to live. They always want to know how we do it. However, we stumble over answering that question because there is no simple answer to give in just a few sentences. We do not have jobs or just one business. We also hate the idea of being defined by what we do for a living. There is much more to life than just working and making money!

This book is the answer to that question. It's our goal to share with you how we created a lifestyle that allows us to live life on our terms.

The Anti Suit Entrepreneur is a concept that represents what we (and many other people) do to live life on our terms. Simply put, the Anti Suit Entrepreneur is about escaping mediocrity so you can live life on your terms.

There are four main areas to the Anti Suit Entrepreneur.

Living life on your terms - to escape the void of mediocrity that infects so many people living in first world countries and to replace that void with what you truly want out of life.

Income streams - to pay the bills and fund your life. More than one stream of income will provide financial security as well.

Flexible schedule - to have complete control over your schedule, have time to take advantage of various opportunities, be spontaneous in having f u n   a n d doing what you want, when you want.

Entrepreneurial ethos - to embrace the beliefs of being an entrepreneur. Become an entrepreneur to make things happen for yourself, develop mental toughness, and become self sufficient so you never have to rely on a boss or a corporation for a paycheck.

The first letters of those four points spell out LIFE. Hopefully every time you say, read or hear the word *life*, you will think of those four points. Our intent is to burn those points into your mind. Constant reminders about those four points will help you become an Anti Suit Entrepreneur.

Living Life on Your Terms

Living life on your terms means something different to everyone. There is no one size fits all. So we are not going to try and dictate what your life should be like. After all, it is *your* life.

We both started our Anti Suit Entrepreneur journeys independently of each other. However, many of our goals and interests are similar and that eventually led us to crossing paths, becoming friends and business partners.

To us, wearing a suit and tie every day epitomizes the exact opposite of living life on our terms. The suit and tie represent so many of the things associated with living a life of mediocrity. To Chris, it is commuting, answering to a boss, and having zero control over his schedule. To Jason, it is working endless hours at the law firm, stressing out over cases and employees. Every morning as he got dressed, putting on a tie felt like putting a noose around his neck.

We asked, "What value and function do the suit and tie bring into the workplace?" Beyond simple fashion and being the norm, they add nothing. Wearing a suit and tie does not magically make you more productive and better at your job. Wearing them is just what you are supposed to do in the business world. The sticking point for us is that many of the most successful and wealthiest people never wear a suit and tie.

Why should we wear a suit and tie? We never got a good reason why and still have not! We decided to ditch the suit and tie. Ditching them represented freedom to us: choosing what clothes to wear, not wasting time in rush hour, not fighting with bosses, not dealing with office politics, and setting our own schedules for our lives. In some ways we became more productive and profitable because we were happier with our situations.

Our disdain for wearing a suit and tie is the origin of the Anti Suit Entrepreneur concept. The Anti Suit became a symbol to us of living life on our terms. We want the Anti Suit concept to be a reminder for you about living like on *your* terms. Does this mean you have to stop wearing a suit and tie? No, it doesn't. If wearing a suit and tie (or professional clothing) is enjoyable to you, then do it! Quite a few people we know feel empowered by wearing a power suit or putting on business high heels. Remember, it is your life. You just need to figure out your terms and then start living them.

Just to be clear, we are not the jerks that show up to weddings or black tie events wearing board shorts and sandals; we dress properly to show appropriate respect at certain occasions.

Income Streams & Flexible Schedule

Income streams and a flexible schedule go hand-in-hand. Often people have a lot of one and very little of the other, or very little of both.

Before Jason became an Anti Suit Entrepreneur, he was making a lot of money, but had very little flexibility and freedom in his schedule. In his seven years of running a very successful law firm in Northern California, he opened up two new offices in neighboring cities. It was stressful, hectic, and very time consuming running a business of that size! Jason thought to himself, "What good is making all this money if I can't use it to enjoy life. I want freedom now, not 40 years from now when I retire!" In the back of his mind, he knew that many lawyers died of heart attacks at fairly young ages because of stress.

Before Chris became an Anti Suit Entrepreneur, he was so distraught at the thought of commuting hours every day to work at a job, that he considered completely dropping out of the professional world and becoming a white water rafting guide. He would have extreme flexibility in his schedule but almost no money. That would be great for a year or two, but what would life be like in 10 or 20 years after living that lifestyle with no money? That outcome was not attractive either!

As we became Anti Suit Entrepreneurs, we were able to develop both a good income and a flexible schedule, two things which are frequently contradictory to each other. Generally, as one goes up, the other goes down. However, it is possible to have both. We are walking proof of it!

Is having both good income and a flexible schedule a cake walk? No, it is not. It takes effort and hard work to develop them. As you probably know, anything worthwhile takes hard work. In many aspects, though, it does not take any more effort than what many people do by devoting years to a degree or working up the corporate ladder.

While living in the first world can bring a life of mediocrity, it also presents many new and unique opportunities for becoming an Anti Suit Entrepreneur. The reason many people perceive the Anti Suit Entrepreneur lifestyle as being very difficult to achieve is because of their mindset. That's where developing the entrepreneurial ethos comes into play.

Entrepreneurial Ethos

As you know, a college degree no longer equals a good job, let alone any job at this point. Companies no longer take care of their employees as they used to. It's no longer: get a job with a good company, work 40 years with them, and retire comfortably with a company pension. Companies are constantly outsourcing jobs to other countries and replacing workers with technology. There is no longer that unspoken agreement between companies and employees of "Work hard for us and we'll be loyal to you and take care of you." There are only a few companies that still have that attitude. But, here's the problem: How long will that last? What happens when the CEO retires or the business gets bought out by a big corporation that doesn't have the same values? What happens then?

This change in the economy is why you must embrace the entrepreneurial ethos! Whether you are aware of it or not, everyone needs to be an entrepreneur today. Typically when people think of an entrepreneur, they conjure up Bill Gates, Richard Branson, and other billionaire business owners. However, according to the Merriam-Webster Dictionary, the definition of entrepreneur is "one who organizes, manages, and assumes the risks of a business or enterprise." An entrepreneur assumes all the risks and takes all responsibility for starting and running a business. While those famous examples pop into many people's minds, risk and responsibility are what really define an entrepreneur.

The Anti Suit Entrepreneur is about taking that same concept and applying it to your life. Replace the word "business" with "life" and you get "one who organizes, manages, and assumes the risks of his or her life." That attitude and mindset are exactly what you need in this new economy.

Do college degrees "take care of you" with a guaranteed job? **No.**

Does a corporation "take care of you" with a job for all your working years? **No.**

Is the government going to protect your job from getting outsourced? **No.**

Is the government going to take care of you in your retirement years? **No.**

So, who or what is going to take care of you? **You!** It falls on your shoulders to take care of yourself. It's up to you to assume all the risks and responsibilities for your life because no one else will. Just as an entrepreneur is responsible for everything in a business, you are responsible for everything in your life.

We are not saying that you must become the next Mark Zuckerberg or even start your own business. The point we are stressing is that you must embrace the entrepreneurial ethos so you can take care of yourself and family; no one else is going to.

"You're Crazy, Chris..."

Embracing the entrepreneurial ethos is probably the hardest area for people to develop. It was for Chris. Growing up, Chris was always told to get good grades in school so he could get into a good college and then get a good, secure job that paid well. That's what he did.

He graduated with a GPA above a 4.0 from high school, scored extremely high on the SAT's, and even received letters of interest from a couple of very prestigious Ivy League schools. Good grades - **check**.

He decided to attend Virginia Tech University because of its very inexpensive in-state tuition, its Corps of Cadets military program, and its top notch engineering school. Good college - **check**.

As with many college students, things changed for Chris while at college. He realized engineering was not his real interest as he thought it was all throughout high school. He did not pursue a military career as he had planned for a variety of reasons.

As a fall back, getting a degree from the business school seemed like a good idea. He quickly realized that business school wasn't really teaching him anything about running or working in a business. A lot of it focused on how to get a job by interviewing, networking with potential employers, and setting expectations of working for 10 different companies over his lifetime. Good Job - **not there**.

"Shit! What now?" Chris wondered. Chris saw the writing on the wall that relying on a job as his parents' generation did, wasn't going to cut it. Since it was clear to Chris that a job was not the way to go, that realization backed him into reading about entrepreneurship. And he got addicted to the entrepreneurship ethos.

He started devouring every book on the topic, attending seminars, and starting a variety of side businesses while still in school. He thought about dropping out to pursue entrepreneurship, but decided against that. However, his main focus while attending school became entrepreneurship and not his studies, much to dismay of his parents and the bewilderment of his friends.

"Chris, you've got so much going for you, why are you 'throwing it away'? You're crazy for doing that!" people said in so many words to him. Chris tried to explain why, but no one really seemed convinced. But it didn't matter; Chris saw the writing on the wall for disappearing "good jobs" and was bitten by the idea of becoming an Anti Suit Entrepreneur. Now, he went through his doubts, second (and third, fourth and fifth!) guesses at himself, and through miserable failures at businesses he started. But his gut kept telling him that the Anti Suit Entrepreneur path was the way to go. It's a good thing he listened to his gut, too, because when he graduated in 2005, he didn't need to get a job and he soon moved to Miami's South Beach. And he's never had a job since.

He embraced the entrepreneur ethos during the 2002 - 2005 time frame, well before the Great Recession that started in 2008. After the Great Recession, it became obvious to many that "good jobs" were a thing of the past. For many, it was now about getting "any job," let alone a "good job."

People now understood the path Chris had chosen and why. The path (and Chris) did not look so crazy anymore, especially since the majority of people were in mediocre jobs that they flat out hated and were drowning in student debt. People had fallen into the trap of living a life of mediocrity. Many wanted out.

The New Rules

Since the Great Recession, we are constantly bombarded with questions on how we escaped a life of mediocrity and became Anti Suit Entrepreneurs. Most people want a "1, 2, 3, A, B, C" step-by-step checklist with guaranteed results by a certain deadline. That checklist simply doesn't exist. Every person and situation is different.

We never had a step-by-step checklist to becoming an Anti Suit Entrepreneur, but we still achieved that goal. We kept asking ourselves, "What did we do that helped get us here? What did we do that did *not* help us get here?" We reflected on our past to answer those questions.

Eleven themes kept popping up. Over the years, the cumulative effect of these eleven themes added up to us living the Anti Suit Entrepreneur lifestyle. We now refer to these as the New Rules of LIFE. It's our sincere belief that these New Rules are becoming what a college degree was 50 years ago, which is almost guaranteed success.

"$50,000/Year to $50,000/Month in 90 Days!"

How many websites and online ads have you seen that basically promise to teach you how to "get rich quickly while being lazy and putting everything on autopilot by using automated software and outsourcing your life and business to India for $17 a day"?

How many books have you seen or read that promise to teach you the "secrets of real estate investing with $0 down and not having to invest any of your own money, while using a 'fool proof' system that guarantees your success"?

We could make a list that goes on and on, but you probably get the point. If you're like us, you've seen hundreds of them. You've also probably purchased a few of those products yourself. We have over the years, out of hope and curiosity.

They all had one thing in common; **they were complete B.S.** They all sold the hope of attaining "easy riches while doing almost no work by working smarter, not harder." In reality, they usually just sold another course or seminar that would teach you the 'real secrets.' The new course was usually 10 to 50 times more than what you just paid for the current product!

To us, a lot of those authors and self-proclaimed "wealth gurus" are borderline scam artists. How often are they trying to sell the next "game changer" that will solve all of your financial worries and woes? It makes you wonder where they are really making their money, doesn't it?

Here's the bottom line; there is no formula or recipe for overnight success or getting rich quickly. The New Rules covered in this book will not make you an overnight success. We wish they did, but they don't. If we were to say otherwise, we'd just be selling you a shovel full of B.S.

We can promise you this: that the New Rules, if you apply them, will help you start living your LIFE and becoming an Anti Suit Entrepreneur. But it won't happen overnight. It takes work, dedication, and time to develop and create your LIFE. It's like working out and getting into shape. You don't go to the gym for five days and magically get the body you want. It takes consistency, time, planning, and changes in nutrition to achieve that body. The longer you do it, the better you get and the faster the results start happening.

The same is true for the New Rules.

Are You Suffering From New-itis?

New-itis is not a new thing from which people are suffering. However, all the information that the Internet makes available to people has accentuated how many more people are suffering from new-itis.

New-itis is the term we use for people's desire, need, or even addiction to always moving onto the "next thing" or "newest thing" without ever implementing or applying what they have just learned or read.

One of our businesses helps small business owners with online marketing, sales training, and the creation of short personal commercials through online, self-paced courses. Essentially we took our combined 20+ years of business, sales, and marketing knowledge and created in-depth courses to teach people what we do in business and how we became successful. The main courses contain over 50 hours worth of content spread over about 150 videos. Each course has very specific instructions and exercises to follow. When you complete the course and hopefully the exercises, you should be able to produce a 30 second commercial and online marketing strategy.

About nine out of ten people who go through the entire training, blow through it in one to two weeks and then ask us, "Guys, that training was great! So, what's next?"

We always ask them, "What's your online marketing strategy? What's your 30 second commercial?" and many other questions that relate directly back to the courses and their business! Almost like clockwork, they can't answer the questions. We've noticed that people see all the courses available to them and get focused on "checking them all off" their to-do list as quickly as possible, rather than taking the time to go carefully through them. People who get into that "checking them all off" the to-do list mode often times don't learn anything from the course. This approach is a typical new-itis situation because most of the time what causes this is the need to move on to the next thing. Once people are made aware of this, the light bulb goes on, and then they restart all the training with a new focus: actually learning and applying the information shared.

We are by no means immune to new-itis. Over the years we've been infected, too. Once we learned and identified it, it happened less often. We actually started getting more done and achieving better results in our lives and businesses, too! Other people get similar results.

Stop and think for a minute; how often do you burn through things just to get them done and cross them off the to-do list? How often do you feel the need to move onto the "next best thing" as quickly as possible? How often does new-itis infect you?

We don't want this book to be just another victim of new-itis! We actually want you to learn something here.

Applying the New Rules

You'll notice that at the end of each chapter there is a Anti Suit Entrepreneur Charge Ahead Homework section. Those sections are there to help you apply the New Rules and guide you as you build your LIFE as an Anti Suit Entrepreneur.

The Charge Ahead Homework consists of additional resources, questions, and exercises. Each section will link to a corresponding part of the Anti Suit Entrepreneur website. The Charge Ahead Homework is designed to get you thinking and taking action. It also consists of what has helped us over the years, which will hopefully help you.

It's impossible for any book, course, or person to tell you what is best for your life or exactly what you need to do. Years ago, Chris went to a personal development seminar over a long weekend that was supposed to help the participants break through their personal barriers. There were about 50 people in the audience and one instructor. The instructor shared some great insights and information. At the end of the seminar he told Chris, "Your problem is that you do not take life seriously enough. That's what is stopping you from going to the next level."

That blew Chris away. He always had the attitude that life was just "one big game to play and enjoy." Chris started taking life seriously. It brought boredom, unhappiness, frustration, and a drop in income, the exact opposite of what he expected or wanted!

About six months after that, Chris started trying to figure out what went wrong. He realized that the "taking life seriously" advice was horrible for him! He also started asking himself, "I had no more than five minutes of one-on-one time with the instructor throughout the entire weekend... How the hell is that enough time to evaluate me? It's not!" And as Chris thought about it more and started doing some research, he learned that the instructor had accomplished nothing more in life other than being a personal development instructor. In fact, he was living in a van before he started working with the personal development company. There's nothing wrong with being a personal development instructor, but if it's the only thing a person has accomplished and pays the bills with, what gives him the right to tell someone else how to live his life? It doesn't.

Chris learned two things: (1) Make sure the person you're learning from has some experience to back up what he's saying, and (2) no matter who the person is, **no one knows what's better for your life than you do.** Time and time again we've seen people get screwed up, just as Chris did, because they listen to people, books or seminars that tell them what their problem is and how they need to live life.

You know what's best for you. We do not. That fact is the reason why we created the Charge Ahead Homework Answering. Doing the homework will help you come to realizations and have the proverbial light bulb go on.

Understanding ROI

Return on Investment (ROI) is a formula that allows businesses and investors to measure the potential profitability of a business decision or investment. The ROI concept is at the root of almost every business decision. Businesses and investors are not going to invest money and resources into something if they don't expect a certain amount of money from it.

Let's say ACME, INC has $1,000,000 with which to expand its business. They can invest that money into widgets or gadgets. They estimate that manufacturing and selling widgets would make them $10,000,000 and that gadgets would only make them $5,000,000. That's an easy decision; manufacture the widgets because they will make more money, or have a greater ROI, than if they manufactured gadgets.

In reality, there are a lot more factors and variables that come into play for businesses. Those are out of the scope of this book, since it is not about financial investments. However, the simple example above drives home the point we want: that businesses and investors do an analysis and compare different strategies before making a decision. It's a fundamental decision making process that they are constantly doing.

While it is a fundamental staple in the business world, it's rarely used by individuals. Why is that? Unless a person took business finance classes in college or has read investment books, he was never taught about ROI. The standard business ROI formula doesn't really work for people either. It doesn't measure things like sleeping, eating, and quality of life. You probably need and enjoy those things! Yet, the ROI concept is important for people to understand and apply to their lives. It's a necessity for developing the LIFE you want.

Understanding ROLIFE

Over the years, we've used the ROI concept in all areas of our lives. The problem is that ROI doesn't fit in analyzing the LIFE you want. So, we came up with what we call ROLIFE. It stands for:

Return
On
Living life on your terms
Income streams
Flexible schedule
Entrepreneurial mindset development

Since the Anti Suit Entrepreneur is about developing the LIFE you want, there needed to be a simple way to measure it and help you make decisions. The ROLIFE concept has helped us tremendously over the years. It can help you, too.

In our eyes, it is absurd to not do a ROLIFE on a major life decision. All choices have consequences and long term effects on your life. Now, we're not saying you need to do a big in-depth analysis that takes weeks for every decision you make. You do need to figure out the ROLIFE on major life decisions. As Jason did.

Jason's ROLIFE

When Jason turned 30, he started reflecting on what he had accomplished in life up to that point and what he wanted from the next 30 years of his life. This was a time when he needed to make a decision about starting his career as a lawyer and buying the law firm that he'd been running. The gravity of the decision weighed on his shoulders; buying an established law firm with three offices is not a small decision!

He started calculating his ROLIFE if he bought law firm:

Income Streams - He knew the business inside and out. The ability to make great income was there, especially once he had completed the buyout of the business. The low end was $100,000/year. During the good years, it would be in the multiple six figure range. However, it would also force him into relying on one stream or source for his income.

Flexible Schedule - Flexibility was pretty much non-existent, except for one or two trips planned well in advance (and assuming no emergencies came up right before the trip!). His schedule would be dictated and owned with court deadlines, 8 A.M. hearings with judges, and late night to take care of all the business details.

Entrepreneurial Ethos - Many people would consider running a law firm as an entrepreneurial venture. However, the excitement of expanding the law firm into two nearby cities had worn off. Now, much of running the business was like running an "adult day care," because it felt he was babysitting employees and dealing with overinflated egos of various lawyers. He saw the writing on the wall that he'd never be able to step away from the law firm and have it run without him there. It felt as though he was a buying a job with a $50,000/mo overhead! Jason realized he enjoyed the challenges and creativity it takes to get a business up and running and making it successful, yet he was ready for a new challenge.

Living life on his terms - His life would be spent following terms laid out by the court system and running the business! Having time to pursue his own interests seemed nearly impossible. He had no problem with sacrificing in the short term, but he didn't see that as being possible with the law firm. Ultimately, Jason didn't see himself being happy going down that path.

Jason was looking at his next 30 years with only one out of four areas in his favor. Yes, he could make great money, but was that worth sacrificing the other three areas of his LIFE: the ROLIFE wasn't there for him. Yet, this was no easy decision because he knew the business so well, could make great money at it, and was in his comfort zone.

His gut kept telling him he needed to move in a different direction, that if he didn't, down the road, he'd be unhappy and regretful of his decision. The problem is that he had no idea what direction to take. However, he knew that he didn't want to stay on his current path. This dilemma was the beginning of Jason's journey to becoming an Ant-Suit Entrepreneur and living LIFE.

Compare the Opportunity Cost

The New Oxford American Dictionary defines opportunity cost as "the loss of potential gain from other alternatives when one alternative is chosen." Every decision you make has a "cost" to it because you can't enjoy the benefits or reap the rewards from other alternatives. Opportunity cost is an economic term; that's why the definition is so abstract. However, it's a powerful concept that goes with ROLIFE.

When you go down one path in life or make a major career or education decision, you're giving up other options. Each option has its own pros and cons. That's why we recommend calculating ROLIFE for the current path you're on and, if possible, for each alternative.

We can already hear you saying, "I don't have any alternatives or know enough about them to calculate ROLIFE!" We understand what you're thinking because we've been in your shoes.

Start Identifying Your Anti List

Generally we're taught to figure out what we want and then start working toward it. However, we have found it much easier to start with what you do *not* want. That's why we created the Anti List. The Anti List has been one of our secrets to accomplishing a lot in life and business. It's been a cornerstone for us in developing the LIFE that we each wanted.

The idea behind the Anti List is very simple; write down what you hate, do not like, and do not want in your life. Write out what you're against or anti about. This process is exactly what we did that led us to becoming Anti Suit Entrepreneurs.

Over the years, we've found that this concept is the easiest place for us and the majority of the people that we've mentored to start. Think about it; most people can rattle off what they hate or dislike concisely and without hesitation. Yet, if you ask them what they want, you usually get silence and then a disjointed answer. Clearly identifying what you're anti about gives you a clear starting point because you know what you don't want. This awareness allows you to work backwards into what you do want.

Identifying the areas that you're anti about will help ensure that you do not slowly fall into mediocrity. Anytime you start going down a path that leads to your Anti List, warning bells will go off, urging you to readjust and make changes before you get too far down that path.

Keep Moving Forward

This quote from Steve Jobs sums up what to do once you've created your Anti List:

"You can't connect the dots looking forward; you can only connect them looking backwards. So you have to trust that the dots will somehow connect in your future. You have to trust in something — your gut, destiny, life, karma, whatever. This approach has never let me down, and it has made all the difference in my life."

After we created our Anti List, we just kept moving forward. We kept reading books, self reflecting, seeking out people for guidance, and exploring new areas. Often times it felt as though we were fumbling in the dark, but we just kept moving forward, a process that eventually led to "many of the dots getting connected."

Our goal is to have the New Rules of LIFE help you in connecting the dots. At the end of the book, we'll recommend some different alternatives to explore that may help you become an Anti Suit Entrepreneur. We're saving those for the end, so you have all the New Rules of LIFE as a foundation and starting point.

We put this New Rule first because as you start learning and implementing the other New Rules, you'll need to evaluate which ones to focus on first. You'll need to prioritize.

ANTI SUIT
CHARGE AHEAD
HOMEWORK

Get it. Read it. **Apply it.**

Register for the Anti Suit Entrepreneur Online Seminar Series, which includes a seminar on this chapter, *Live Life on Your Terms* at www.AntiSuitEntrepreneur.com/chapter1

Chapter 2
The New College Degree

In real estate, you've heard it is all about "location, location, and location." To the Anti Suit Entrepreneur, it's all about "skills, skills, and skills." **Money Making Skills to be exact.**

Money Making Skills are skills that allow a person to generate income without having to rely on an employer or other people. It's about you having 100% control over your ability to make money and take care of yourself, no matter what the economy or job market is doing. This control falls in line with embracing the entrepreneurial ethos (the "E" from LIFE.)

For many people, this is a major paradigm shift because we're taught to get an education, find a job, and rely on a paycheck. That philosophy used to work, but not anymore. It's a carryover from when college degrees equaled high paying jobs, employers actually treated their employees as people, and stable jobs were available. We don't need to cover all the statistics and horror stories about layoffs, job outsourcing, and college graduates moving back in with their parents. As the job market and economy have shifted to a more global economy, at a time resulting in treating workers as commodities, there has been a lag in people successfully transitioning because the philosophy of relying on a job for income has been so ingrained in people's minds.

Since a college degree no longer guarantees a job, having Money Making Skills is the new college degree!

Confidence and Peace of Mind

A major benefit to having Money Making Skills is that it gives you an incredible amount of confidence in yourself and peace of mind. We've had friends get laid off, get stuck in a job they don't like but have no other options, and not have enough money to live life on their terms. Every time that has happened, it's made us appreciate the Money Making Skills that we developed over the years. In fact, it's given us a great amount of confidence and peace of mind because we know we'll never be in that situation.

Anytime we've needed to increase our income, we've been able to. We don't have to ask for a raise, or get a second job, or spend three years earning an MBA at night school. We simply did more with our Money Making Skills and made more money! We did it all on our own. Now, it didn't happen overnight. It took planning and time to make more money. But we did it 100% on our own, without having to rely on any employer, company, or anyone else. How many can do that? Can you?

All of our income and businesses could disappear and we would have no problem getting back on our feet and generating a good income in a relatively short amount of time. We hope that never happens, but if it does, we are fully capable because of the Money Making Skills we have developed.

Having Money Making Skills has removed a lot of stress from our lives, worry about the future, and sleepless nights wondering about finances. A lack of all that stress has helped us live happier and healthier lives. There's a big link between financial stress and happiness and health.

What Money Making Skills Should You Learn?

Hopefully you're excited about the idea of developing Money Making Skills. Most people are as they learn about it. Immediately they ask, "What Money Making Skills should I learn?" You're probably asking the same question. We'll share with you the main Money Making Skills that we've learned, but we want to make it clear that you don't need to do exactly what we do or follow those skills exactly. The Money Making Skills fit our personalities and areas of interest. They may or may not fit yours.

One of the upsides to the global and changing economy is that there are numerous Money Making Skills that you can learn. It takes all types of personalities and areas of interest to keep the economy moving forward. We are confident in saying that no matter what your education, background, personality, or areas of interest are, you can develop Money Making Skills.

Are all Money Making Skills the same? No, of course not! Some will make you more money than others. Some are easier and quicker to learn than others. The total money you can make is not the number one goal. It's about making money in something that you enjoy while living life. We don't want to see you develop Money Making Skills and then fall into a life of mediocrity because you don't like what you're doing! However, there is one Money Making Skill that you and everyone need to develop...

Communication is #1

"I'll do whatever as long as I don't have to present in front of the class" was a very common phrase that Chris heard over and over during group projects while working on his undergraduate degree. No matter what class or group he was with, people were petrified of standing up in front of the class and giving a ten minute presentation on the group project. People would volunteer to do all the work, create the Powerpoint slides, and even write up the notecards, just so they wouldn't have to present! Usually that meant they were taking on 10 to 40 hours worth of school work to avoid ten minutes in front of the class. Chris always volunteered to be the group presenter. He wasn't a fan of standing up in front of the class either, but if it would save hours of work for himself, it was worth the discomfort of ten minutes in front of people.

That anecdote was used because most people can relate to group projects from either high school or college. In our experience, the job of presenting was always the most hated role. It also highlights the number one Money Making Skill: Communication.

Communication is "number one" in our book because everything revolves around it, and the majority of people are afraid of it, not good at it, or both! Those two reasons create value and demand for people who are effective communicators. Communication creates a lot of opportunity to make a lot of money.

The communication Money Making Skill encompasses many areas: sales, negotiating, relationship building, and leadership, to name a few of the big ones. We put all of those areas under the communication umbrella because they are all interconnected and require different forms of communication. You can't do any of those areas unless you're good at communication.

Think about all the great visionaries over the years in the business world. They didn't become great visionaries just because of their ideas. They became great because they could communicate their ideas to people around them and get others to buy into their vision and make it a reality.

Why You Need Communication

You can have great Money Making Skills, but if you can't communicate what you do and why you're good at it, you're going to have a hard time making money. If a person or company doesn't understand what you do and value your work, they will go with someone else or pay you a lot less than you're worth. "Your work will speak for itself" doesn't cut it either. First, you need to get your work or portfolio in front of the person, which isn't always easy. You need communication for it. Second, you need to work with the client or group as you go back and forth to finish the project. You need communication for that.

One of our businesses creates websites and marketing strategies for small businesses. Many times we have to "save the client from himself or herself." The small business client gets fixated on having a certain color, photo, or look to the website. We know that their idea would hurt the website or marketing results. We have to explain this to the client, which is often a tricky process. We can't just steamroll the client and tell them "no." We also can't just do what he or she wants because we know it's not the best thing for the business. Guess what? We use our communication Money Making Skill. Our clients understand why we're making the recommendation; they get a better website and marketing plan, we get fewer issues down the road because they are getting results, and we also get more referrals. We wouldn't be able to accomplish all of the above, if we were not good communicators.

Even if you don't start your own business and you work for someone else, you still need to develop good communication skills. If you don't let the company know what you're doing for it, you'll be skipped over for promotions, new projects, and raises. You may also be on the chopping block when a round of layoffs happens because you're not a key employee.

Perception is Reality

Whatever a person perceives (accurate or inaccurate) is his or her reality. Understanding this concept is extremely important. You need to make sure the person or company gets the "right" picture of you and your work. If they don't, they will form their own perception or someone else will form it for them. And it probably won't add up to the "right" picture.

Unfortunately, there are a lot of people out there who will do whatever it takes to look good and get ahead. They won't hesitate one second to throw you under the bus, if it advances them forward. It's pretty hard to get people like that completely out of your life. Often times you don't know a person is like that until they do it to you. There's no way you can completely prevent that from happening, but that doesn't mean you're helpless. The best way to protect yourself is to be proactive in communicating your value and the type and quality of work you are able to do. Being proactive ensures that others' perceptions of you are correct and helps negate false and misleading statements being said about you.

It's important that you're helping people get the "right" perception of you so they form the "right" reality. This idea makes some people uncomfortable because they feel wrong or manipulative about it. You need to get over that feeling because there is nothing wrong about speaking up for yourself. In fact, you have an obligation to make sure that people around you have the "right" perception about you. Making sure of this "right" perception will help you make more money and be happier. There is nothing more frustrating and unfair than seeing less qualified people having more success than you or getting work that should have been yours.

"I'm Not Good at Communication..."

We both have said "I'm not good at communication (or sales)" when we first started down the path of becoming Anti Suit Entrepreneurs. The reality is that no one is born a great communicator or salesman. Communication is not a genetic trait like height or athletic body type. It's a skill that is learned and developed over the years. Some people appear as if they're a "born salesperson." That couldn't be farther from the truth. They either learned that skill or grew up in an environment that fostered it. Maybe some people got lucky and were born to parents who taught them communication skills. We don't have control over the past. You do have control over learning communication.

When Chris was five, his enunciation skills were so bad that only his parents could understand him. He basically spoke his own language. He was born with fluid in his ears that didn't properly drain. The fluid effectively made him deaf for the first few months of his life, a crucial language formation period. He missed out on hearing the important sounds of the world around him. Ear tubes were eventually put in to drain the fluid. This problem caused Chris to start school a year late and to go through several years of speech therapy.

By the age of eight, he was able to speak normally. Do you think this situation caused confidence issues for him? You bet! There were also quite a few residual issues with certain word pronunciations and jumbling of words. Yet, Chris overcame those residual and self confidence issues when he started becoming an Anti Suit Entrepreneur because he knew the importance of communication.

If you're not confident in your communication abilities or are not good at them, you need to get better. It's that simple. Communication is too important an area to skip over. If you can't communicate how good you are at doing the other Money Making Skills, they probably won't make you money!

Internet Marketing Money Making Skills

At the writing of this book and looking back over the last 10 years, Internet marketing has been one of the most common areas that new entrepreneurs wanted to tackle as a part of their road to entrepreneurship; so, learning how to market on the Internet as a Money Making Skill probably doesn't come as a surprise. However, this fact might: One of the reasons most people fail at Internet marketing is because they are poor communicators. We always tell people, "If you can't sell to someone sitting across a coffee table from you, you won't be able to sell on the Internet." The Internet is just another way for people to communicate with each other on a grand scale. If you can't sell to a person across the coffee table, you're not going sell on a massive scale on the Internet. The Internet is not a magical platform that makes everything easier (despite what many courses say!). The Internet will magnify your skills or lack thereof. At the end of the day, all the information on the Internet was created by a person sitting at a computer somewhere.

Think about your recent Google searches. You probably clicked onto different websites until you found one that gave you the information you wanted. Maybe it was the first website, maybe it was the twentieth, maybe you didn't find the information you wanted. The owner of the website was communicating information to you by text, video, images, or audio. If you were looking to buy something, the website either communicated what the product or service did and sold you on it, or it didn't. If it did, you bought. If it didn't, you hit the back button and went somewhere else.

The websites that sell and make money are the ones that are in touch with people's emotions, problems, hot buttons, interests, worries, and concerns, and so on! They connect with the person on a level that grabs his attention. A big part of becoming a successful Internet Marketer is finding out this type of information about people and communicating to them that your product or service is exactly what they need, so they take out their wallet and buy from you. We firmly believe the best way to find out that information is by communicating with people directly (across the coffee table, over the phone, using Social Media, etc.).

Common Pitfalls

While the Internet is a great way for legitimate people to make money and grow their business, it's also a great way for scam artists to make money as well. Since the Internet is still a young technology that very few people (consumers and law enforcement) understand, these scam artists can really rake people (and their wallets) over the coals. Let's cover a few of the common pitfalls that separate people from their money.

If it sounds too good to be true, it probably is. It seems that every week a new course is popping up that promises to show you the "secret loopholes in Google that will allow you to make $100,000+ in 60 days." Trust us, these are complete B.S. Let's say, for argument's sake, that there really is a "secret loophole that can make you $100,000 in 60 days," do you really think someone would sell it for $39?

These $100,000 in 60 days for $39 "opportunities" often involved pre-made template websites. **These pre-made, cookie cutter websites or landing pages don't work anymore.** They did about 10 years ago. But not today! The majority of search engines and advertising platforms have banned those types of sites from appearing. Many Internet surfers are also fatigued of these websites and largely ignore them now because of previous bad experiences or seeing 20,000 similar websites. Many affiliate programs fall into this category. Affiliate marketing can work, but not with the prefab websites that most offer.

No transparency. This one gets a lot of people. Many of these "scammy" websites have no contact details, privacy policy, terms and conditions, and ways to get your questions answered **before you buy their course.** Any legitimate website is going to have its address, a contact email, a contact phone number, a privacy policy, and terms and conditions, at the minimum. The most important thing is to determine if there is a way to communicate with a person at the website to get your questions answered. The website owner probably doesn't post his cell phone number on the website, but there should be a way for you to get in touch with him or her via phone, email, or social media. If you don't get a response or you get a lousy response, that should raise a red flag and tell you to move on to somewhere else.

"Only 97 19 copies left!' This is just flat out lying if the person is selling a digital product. Once a digital product (eBook or eCourse) is created, it can be downloaded an unlimited number of times! It's not as though they had to hire a printer to do the job. If a website only has a certain number of eBooks left, you need to hit the back button and go somewhere else because they are just lying to you. Now, if the website is selling physical products or slots for coaching, then that's legitimate because there is a finite number of those.

High pressured sales tactics. Many websites will have someone call you to sell you on a high ticket item that costs a few thousand to $20,000 or more. If the person is asking you, "How much room do you have on your credit cards?" or "How much you can put down today?", that should raise a red flag. The rule of thumb is that if you ever get the "You must buy today to take advantage of this offer," you need to hang up the phone or click away from the website immediately!

Endless upsells. An upsell is when a website or company offers another product or service to purchase after you just purchased something. An upsell is not necessarily a bad thing by itself. It's when the website gives you the upsells that seem to never end. A typical example is selling an eBook for $19 to $49 dollars, then upselling a product for between $200 to $400, then another product around the $1,000 price point, and then a big ticket item (seminars or coaching) for $3,000 to $10,000.

Outrageous bonuses! Bonuses are a legitimate way to get people buying from a website. But when bonuses get outrageous, that should raise a red flag. Often time we'll see promotions of new informational products that cost $49 and come with over $2,000 in bonuses of PDF downloads and videos. If a website constantly has these outrageous bonuses, that should make you think twice about how valuable the information is. If the bonuses were really worth $2,000... why wouldn't they sell them for $2,000?

The Big 3: What it Really Takes to Make Money on the Internet

The Internet is constantly evolving. Some marketing techniques that worked great years ago are ineffective today. We're into simplifying and getting the maximum return possible on anything we do. We focus on what we call the Big 3 for our Internet marketing.

Content

Content is king. If you have studied any Internet marketing, you've probably heard that phrase before. It's absolutely true. Simply put, content is stuff on your website. It's the reason people go there! A website cannot exist without content. Content is information delivered in text, image, audio, video, or a combination of those things. Content is why people visit websites. If a website has good content that is relevant to what the person is looking for, he'll stay on the site. Good content and design can lead to a sale, repeat visits, downloading an eBook, and other profitable results. Think about the websites you visit regularly. What keeps you going back? Content, that is relevant to you, keeps you coming back!

Traffic

People have to find your website in order for you to make money. Think of a traditional retail store that has amazing products at amazing prices that is built in the middle of nowhere and people don't know about it. If people don't know it exists and cannot find it, it doesn't matter how great the products or prices are! The same is true on the

Internet. Getting traffic to a website can be very tricky and is way out of the scope of this book. Many companies spend hundreds of thousands to millions of dollars in order to get traffic to their website.

Relationships

Every year, the Internet has become more and more about relationships. Years ago, many people built successful websites with just traffic and content. In today's Internet, you must focus on relationship building. We're not just talking about having a Facebook or Twitter presence. No, we're talking about actively engaging people to come to your website and build relationships with every person possible. People buy from people they know, like, and trust. Relationship building can take on many forms. It's impossible to email or call every single person that comes to your website. Have you ever read a book or watched a series of videos and feel as though you know the author? That is relationship building at its finest. That's what successful Internet marketers are doing. The smart ones then take it up a notch and try their best to communicate or engage people one-on-one by answering questions, replying to Facebook posts, and emailing back and forth.

Which Big 3 technique is the most important? They are all interrelated. It's hard to have success on the Internet without all three in place. You can't drive traffic to your website until you have content. You can't build relationships with people if they can't find you (traffic.) Below is a graphic that we use in some of our Internet marketing courses to show how they work together.

MONETIZATION

"T" stands for traffic. "R" stands for relationships. "C" stands for content. Below the Big 3 Triangle, we have the word monetization. Monetization is how you plan on making money from your website and Internet marketing efforts. There are numerous ways to monetize your website, such as products, affiliate marketing, eBooks, eCourses, software, and lead generation. The Big 3 will help you make the most money with your Internet marketing skills and website.

We wanted to share with you the big picture on what makes a successful Internet Marketer. With Internet marketing, "the devil is in the details." We could write an entire series of books on Internet marketing alone. Since this book is about helping you become an Anti Suit Entrepreneur, we'll stop writing about Internet Marketing and keep moving.

A Million Dollar Part-Time Skill

Jason stumbled upon a Money Making Skill that has helped him make over a million dollars on his road to Anti Suit Entrepreneurship. While attending law school, Jason got the urge to learn about and teach himself computer programming. He didn't have a specific money or business goal to achieve by learning computer programming, but he had a strong desire to do so and figured it would come in handy down the road. It most certainly did!

Jason purchased a book about ColdFusion, which is a computer programming language. He started reading it during the boring law school lectures. Most of his classmates thought he was crazy for not focusing 100% on law school. Jason ignored them and kept studying the ColdFusion programming book because the Internet boom was going on, and he figured it would come in handy at some point his life, regardless of what he did. Fast forward a few years later to when Jason decided to not purchase the law firm and rather go down the path of becoming an Anti Suit Entrepreneur.

The first business he started was a nutrition business. He chose to focus on nutrition because he had a strong belief in what proper nutrition can do for people. Today you see countless ads and websites marketing nutritional products on the Internet. Back when Jason got started, very few people were using the Internet to market nutritional products. His programming Money Making Skill came in very handy because he was able to build websites and then eventually a marketing and sales system that allowed him to successfully build his nutrition business.

He built his business into a very significant income. In fact, the nutrition business replaced the income he would have made from the law firm. The nutrition business is what gave Jason the Anti Suit Entrepreneur lifestyle because he didn't have to answer to a boss, wear a suit, or get up at a certain time. He worked hard, but he did it on his terms.

The New College Degree

Jason's learning how to program is a prime example of why learning Money Making Skills is the New College degree. The programming book cost Jason less than $50. However, some law schools cost well over $100,000 for three years. When you think about it, isn't it mind boggling that a $50 investment in a book ended up helping Jason make more money than most lawyers who invested three years and upwards of a $100,000?

Getting a law degree used to guarantee a job and a decent salary, but not anymore. In fact, there have been numerous lawsuits by recent law school graduates suing their law schools for providing misleading information about job and salary data for graduates. One lawyer, suing a California law school, said recent graduate jobs included "literally folding shirts in Macy's."

One of the problems with the mentality of relying on a degree for a job is that it leaves you dependent on others for a job or income. If you develop Money Making Skills, along with the necessary communication skills, you have control over your ability to take care of yourself and your family. Learning Money Making Skills is a huge part of developing the entrepreneurial ethos (The "E" from LIFE) and becoming an Anti Suit Entrepreneur.

Where to Start

It's important to understand that there's no set or defined plan for you to develop money making skills, like the way college degrees and MBA programs are laid out. You need drive and discipline in order to learn them. Jason had the discipline to study the ColdFusion book on his own and start practicing programming. He had no school or teacher giving him programming assignments or giving him tests to make sure he was learning the material. As you start going down the path of learning Money Making Skills, it's easy to fall into traps of putting off learning them and setting them to the side, since there is no traditional degree-like structure required.

The best way to learn is by "On the job Money Making Skills training." You're familiar with on the job training for a new job. You can learn Money Making Skills in a very similar fashion. With all the changes in the economy, there are ample opportunities to get in a situation where you can make money while actually learning the Money Making Skills. That process usually involves working with a mentor and starting your own business. The rest of the book will discuss those points and have some specific recommendations at the end. The recommendations will make more sense once you have the knowledge foundation of the New Rules of the Anti Suit Entrepreneur.

Developing Money Making Skills will not happen overnight. Many people won't give a second thought to committing four years to a College Degree, yet expect to learn Money Making Skills in a matter of weeks. You don't learn Money Making Skills overnight. It's going to take some time and money to develop Money Making Skills as well. The good news is that you can usually learn these skills in a shorter time frame and for a lot less money than is required for a college degree. Plus, you can usually start making money while still learning, where in college you spend four years before you can start making any money.

In the previous chapter, we talked about ROLIFE. To remind you what it stands for:

Return
On
Living life on your terms
Income streams
Flexible schedule
Entrepreneurial mindset development

You need to carry the ROLIFE concept forward as you start learning Money Making Skills. Don't look at the money you spend on books, seminars, consultants, and courses as an expense, but rather as an investment. Expect to get a return on your investment from the time and money you put into learning a Money Making Skill. Don't just look at how much money you can make, but put it into the perspective of LIFE. Will it make you money and allow you to do what you enjoy?

All of our income and businesses could dry up today, but because we have such a solid set of Money Making Skills, we would be generating income on our own in a matter of weeks. Keep in mind that it's not a matter of *if* you lose income, but a matter of *when*.

We can survive and thrive with our Money Making Skills. Can you?

ANTI SUIT
CHARGE AHEAD
HOMEWORK

Get it. Read it. **Apply it.**

Register for the Anti Suit Entrepreneur Online Seminar Series, which includes a seminar on this chapter, *The New College Degree* at www.AntiSuitEntrepreneur.com/chapter2

Chapter 3
Why Most People Never "Get Ahead"

How much did you really learn about money, finances, insurance and taxes growing up and in school? Probably not much.

The school system doesn't teach anything on these subjects. In some ways, it's mind boggling that schools teach kids subjects like trigonometry or biology, but don't even offer a class on the basics of personal finance to teach people about the basics of managing their personal finances. In many households, it's an avoided subject. Anyone else have memories of parents fighting about money growing up?

One of the reasons people do not get ahead in life is because they are never taught the basics of money. If they don't understand the basics, how can they make smart choices? It's nearly impossible to.

Jason earned a double degree in Accounting and Finance, and Chris earned a degree in Financial Planning. One would think that getting an education in those areas would teach everything you would need to know. As we became Anti Suit Entrepreneurs, we realized that there was a lot more to learn. Those degrees taught us a lot, but often times it was abstract knowledge or information that didn't apply to personal finances and getting ahead in life.

The goal of this chapter is to teach you the financial concepts we have learned over the years, that have helped us become Anti Suit Entrepreneurs, *living life on our terms*. The knowledge from the college degrees and reading various financial and business books helped us. The best knowledge we have learned is from constantly observing what's going on, questioning the status-quo, and applying the KISS (Keep It Simple, Silly) principle. Many of the terms, phrases, and ideas used in the financial world and in many books are abstract and often times get used interchangeably and lead to confusion. Sticking with our common sense approach and keeping the KISS principle in mind, we have developed many of our own phrases. We hope that they will help you understand money and finances as they have helped us over the years.

Cash In, Cash Out: It's That Simple

In the accounting world, assets are anything the corporation owns. These could be land, a factory building, cash in the bank, patents, or intellectual property. In the financial world, assets are claims or contracts to something of value. Examples of financial assets are stocks or bonds. In the eyes of consumers, assets represent their house or their car. Confused? Many people are when we discuss all of that with them. Do not worry about understanding all the different definitions of assets. We shared those definitions with you to make the point of how words get used interchangeably and cause confusion. We haven't even talked about liabilities (the money that you owe!).

Keep it simple with Cash In (CI) and Cash Out (CO). CI means anything that brings cash into your life. CO means anything that takes cash out. Some people think our CI and CO viewpoint is too much of a simplified financial viewpoint for it to be any good. We argue the opposite. Why does something have to be so complicated that it takes years of studying to understand?

This common sense approach helped us avoid the real estate bubble that so many people got caught up in and were ruined by. For decades, people have said, "It's always better to own than to rent. Buying a house will be one of the greatest investments you ever make. Your house is your biggest asset!" We always asked ourselves, "Will buying a house or condo be cash in or cash out?" The answer was CO during many years of the real estate bubble. Whether you rent or own, you'll always be spending money. Our question was, "Which option will be the least amount of CO?" In our eyes, the less money going out the door is less money that you need to bring in!

Chris rented a two bedroom condo in Clearwater Beach, FL for $1,100 a month. To Chris that was a very fair price because it was only a five minute bike ride from the beach, was on the top floor of the building, and had a great view of the water. A few months into his lease, the owner mentioned to Chris that he was going to sell the condo and wanted to give Chris the first option to buy it in order to keep things simple and keep the costs down (no realtors involved, etc.). The potential of owning the condo caught Chris's attention. The owner wanted $385,000 for it. Chris went online to use a mortgage calculator to figure out monthly mortgage payments, property taxes, and insurance costs. The total monthly cost was going to be about $2,800! That included putting $40,000 (10% of the price) down, too! It made no sense to Chris to purchase when it would cost him over three times the amount on a monthly basis while having to put $40,000 down.

The condo had been valued at close to $900,000 during the height of the real estate boom. "Would the value go back up?" Chris wondered at the time. He had no way of knowing if it would. Considering the simple Cash-In (CI), Cash-Out (CO) philosophy, buying the condo didn't make sense. Chris passed on buying it and was sure glad that he did. He moved out a year later to move to Tampa. If he had bought the place, he would have been stuck trying to sell the condo at a loss or renting it out for a big monthly loss. Both options would have caused CO.

Over the years, we've had many married friends start a family where the wife left her job in order to have the baby and raise the kid(s). Going down from two incomes to one, with more mouths to feed and care for, creates stress and hardship. In one case, the wife wanted to go back to work for more CI. However, once they figured in the cost for daycare, gas, car expenses, and everything else, the job would have actually caused more CO! Fortunately, for them, they did a Cash-In, Cash-Out (CICO) analysis before making that decision. Not all of our friends have, and they ended up getting stuck in a situation with more money going out. They also had less time to spend with their children.

We realize that every decision has many factors that can't always be tied back to CICO. Yet, as a general rule of thumb, CICO is a great starting point. We always ask ourselves the question, "Is this going to bring cash in (CI) or cause cash to go out (CO)?" It's a very simple question, but also a very powerful one.

Three Types of Income

We categorize income by how much effort it takes to generate the income <u>and</u> how flexible (or inflexible) the schedule is that is required to generate the income. As Anti Suit Entrepreneurs, making a good income is only as good as your schedule is flexible. If you have read other financial or business books, some of this will be familiar, but we have a different spin on the different types of income.

Active Income

Active income is any income that you actively work toward. If you're not working, you're not making any money.

Active income examples are:

- Hourly wage jobs
- Salaried jobs
- Self employed people (consultants, doctors, lawyers, etc)
- Business owners
- Contract work
- Real estate flipping
- Day trading

Generally speaking, active income requires a lot of effort and affords very little flexibility in your schedule. Some types of active income, such as day trading, offer more flexibility than other types, such as a job. With day trading, you're not making money unless you're actively trading, which often means watching the market throughout the day until a good trade appears. You can make a lot (or lose a lot) of money with day trading or flipping houses, but you still have to be active. If the person is not trading or flipping, he is not making money! We won't spend any more time writing about active income because most people are very familiar with it.

Recurring Income

Recurring income is income that takes effort to get setup and will continue to come in with reduced effort on your part and allow you flexibility in your schedule. Recurring income examples are:

- ‣ Rental property
- ‣ Subscription services
- ‣ Consumable products
- ‣ Business owners
- ‣ Websites that sell products

Many books and people call this type of income residual income and tout how it lasts forever once you've established it. That's simply not the truth. We call it recurring income to be more accurate and differentiate it from residual income. Recurring income can come in while you're doing nothing or minimal work, but it won't last forever. It takes effort to keep it coming in.

Rental property takes effort up front. Researching various neighborhoods, searching for property, buying the property, getting it ready to rent, and then finally finding a tenant is all effort needed up front, before you can make a dime of recurring income. Once the tenant is in there and paying you rent, you're making recurring money with reduced effort and a more flexible schedule, until a toilet gets clogged, the tenant moves out, or the rental property needs work. Now, you need to put more effort in to get that particular task done. You can hire a property manager to deal with the day to day things, but you'll still have to monitor the property manager, make authorizations, and tend to other duties.

Cell phone and cable companies are great examples of subscription services. It's amazing how much money they spend on advertising and reducing up front costs to get people using their service. It's easy to figure out why. It's a hassle to change once you're set up.

One of our businesses is a contact manager and marketing system that many people and businesses pay a monthly fee to use. We put a lot of effort into making it a great system by updating the code to work on the latest devices. However, it also gives us a tremendous amount of flexibility because we're able to work on it when it fits our schedule. Occasionally the server will go down or someone will try to hack the system, and we drop everything to handle the issue. When that happens, our effort and inflexibility of schedule shoots through the roof. Thankfully this happens very rarely and usually only takes a couple of hours to remedy. If we don't address the issue or keep updating the system, our clients will go somewhere that is.

A consumable product is one in which people buy the product, use it up, and then buy more. Gasoline is the perfect example of a consumable product. When you own a car, you have limited choices. You either keep refilling it at the gas station or buy a car that doesn't require gas!

Another area in which we work is the marketing and sales side of the nutrition industry. Nutritional products, in which we're big believers, are consumable products that people use until they are empty or gone and then purchase more to replenish their supply. We've built a very strong recurring income in the nutritional industry. It took a good amount of effort up front. We had to find a product that we would take ourselves and be able to honestly recommend to people. Effort and time were invested into learning about the products, what makes them different from other products out there, who can benefit from them, how to sell them, and getting people on a monthly recurring order. Once people started taking the product, many noticed an improvement in the health and quality of their day-to-day lives, so when the bottle ran out, they wanted to buy some more! Once a person feels the difference, he'll generally stay on the product for a long time, sometimes decades, with minimal effort on our part. Occasionally orders get screwed up, new products come out, or questions come up and we have to put more effort into the business. This business has allowed us a high degree of flexibility in our schedules and a very good recurring income.

It's important to note that a big reason we've built a strong recurring income in the nutrition industry is because we partnered with high quality products. Many people have tried to create recurring income within the nutrition industry, but have failed because of poor quality products. Marketing and sales skills help with getting people to try the product, but the quality of the product is what keeps people ordering again and again. If a customer doesn't feel the difference using the product, he'll most likely stop using it and buy a different product. We bring this point up because it's a great example of why you need a high quality product or service, regardless of your type of business. At the end of the day, if your product or service isn't creating value, then people will go somewhere else. It's hard to build a recurring income if you can't retain customers or clients!

Business owners are listed under both active and recurring income. How the business is setup and run determines what type of income it produces. We have a friend who owns a massage therapy business and is also a tremendous masseuse. But, if he's not in the clinic, he's not making any money because he can't see any clients.

We get so tired of seeing websites and ads that promise you passive or residual income by setting up a website and then letting the sales just flow in! Recently we saw one that talked about how getting your site to the top of Google guaranteed you residual income that would flow in no matter what. First, it's hard to get a website in the number one spot on Google. It's hard to get a website on the first page of Google. It takes a lot of effort to get it there. If you're able to achieve this, you have to do continual work to keep the site at the top of Google and to make sure that people are buying off of your website. If you don't, someone else will knock you off and become "king of the hill!" Having a website that sells can bring in recurring income and give you a flexible schedule, once you put in the effort.

Passive Income

Passive income takes the least amount of effort and gives you the most flexibility in your schedule. Examples of passive income are:

▸ Interest income
▸ Dividend income
▸ Pension income
▸ Social Security income

Passive income is what everyone wants, but it is the hardest to get. Once you get in the position to make passive income, it takes the least amount of effort to maintain.

Interest income is money you make off of your money. Earning interest from money in savings accounts or from money you invested in bonds are examples of interest income. This type of investment allows you to truly sit back, do almost nothing, and have your money work for you and make you more money.

Dividend income is money that you've invested in a business or certain stocks that pay you a percentage of the profits the company makes. The profits shared are known as dividends. You're completely hands off of the business. You are in a completely passive role where you don't have to do any work.

Pension income is money that a company pays you in retirement after working for them for a certain number of years. Pensions are great for retirees because they get a guaranteed income every year until they die. Companies are moving away from pensions because they generally cost the company a lot of money. Pensions are phasing out and are being substituted with 401(k)'s.

Social Security is also a form of passive income, that is, if you can qualify for the ever rising retirement age! Social Security is essentially a pension that is run by the U.S. Government to help retirees. Once a person actually hits the retirement age, he gets Social Security for the rest of his life.

You may be saying, "Earning interest income and dividend income is not something that requires minimal effort because I have to make all that money first!" You're right. The trick is getting that much money saved so you can use it to generate passive income. Once you have the money, it takes almost no effort in order to make passive income with it.

The same train of thought applies to pensions and Social Security. You have to put in decades of work in order to qualify for them. Unfortunately, almost no companies offer pensions anymore. Even if they did, you might have a hard time qualifying for one, since companies hire and fire employees constantly. Social Security is not part of our strategy for creating passive income because we have no idea what the retirement age will be when we approach that age! If it's there, great. If it's not, we will get by fine.

There are other ways to use or invest money to create passive income, but those are out of the scope of this book. The key take away is that passive income requires minimal effort and provides you with the most flexibility in your schedule. In the next chapter, we'll walk you through a roadmap so you can start working toward recurring and passive income. But there are still a few important concepts to cover before moving on.

Leverage: Cash Multiplier

Leverage is using the current resources you have so you can gain more resources with minimum effort. The best way to explain leverage is to walk you through different examples.

Financial Leverage

Financial leverage is the most common use of leverage. It means the use of a small amount of money to control a larger amount of money. The most common example is taking out a mortgage to buy a house. You're using a down payment (typically 5 to 20% of the purchase price) to take out a mortgage. It helps people who would otherwise not be able to buy a house, which is most people. However, leverage is a double edged sword and can go against you as well. In the last decade many people have lost their houses or declared bankruptcy because the value of their house went down, causing them to have a bigger mortgage than the house was worth.

"The stock market will always keep going up! You can't lose money!" is what many people said and believed during the dotcom bubble of the late 90's. Many people took out a second mortgage on their home and then invested it in the stock market. Typically they could borrow money for 5% and were expecting to make returns of 15 to 40%. They were leveraging their home to make money in the stock market. Eventually the dotcom bubble burst and many people lost a lot of money. Some lost all the money they had invested with the money from their second mortgage. Now they had to pay back their second mortgage, but all the money was gone!

A few years ago we got into trading on the foreign exchange market (FX, forex, or currency market) and used financial leverage. The FX market is fairly complicated, so we won't go into all the details. Just understand that the FX market works very similarly to the stock market, but rather than trading stocks, you're trading different countries' currencies, such as the U.S. Dollar or Euro. The FX market is what allows companies and people to do business all around the world. If a person or business located in the U.S. wants to buy something in Europe, the U.S. dollar is converted into Euros so the purchase can take place. The FX market allows that conversion to happen.

People are allowed to trade in the FX market. Essentially the investor is betting that one currency will go up or go down in relation to another currency, just as people bet certain stocks will go up or down. Brokers, who execute the trade, will usually give the investor 50:1 or 100:1 leverage off of his money. For example, if a person puts puts in a $1,000 trade with 100:1 leverage, he's able to control a $100,000 (100 x $1,000) currency trade. This ratio allows the person to make a greater profit, if the currency goes the way he thinks it will. It actually allows the person to make a tremendous amount of money. At the same time, if the currency goes against the person, the leverage can make the person lose not only the $1,000 he put in, but more!

Financial leverage can get very confusing very fast. We won't go into any more details on it. But we did want to touch on different forms because it's incredibly important to know. A combination of banks, investors, and people getting too financially leveraged played a big part in the recent U.S. housing crisis.

Time Leverage

Every person and company has 24 hours in a day. Time leverage allows a person or company to get "more time" and, therefore, make more money. Two ways people and businesses get "more time" are by hiring people or using technology. Both allow more to get done. A lawyer, who just opened up a new practice, needs a secretary or assistant to help with answering phone calls, setting up appointments, and running the office. Even though the lawyer is paying the secretary a salary, he's able to make more money because he can get more work done. While he's in the courtroom, he can't answer the phone when a potential client calls.

Technology is used to help get more done by automating a process and becoming more efficient. Automation allows the person to get work done so more money can be brought in or to save money by hiring fewer employees. Technology ranges from huge car manufacturers automating the assembly line with robots to an individual using software to stay better organized. The more time that a person can create, the more money he will make.

Using this book to share our knowledge on becoming an Anti Suit Entrepreneur gives us time leverage. We had to invest a good chunk of time into writing this book, but it'll greatly save us time. Rather than spending hours explaining the Anti Suit Entrepreneur concepts to people, they can read the book. That will create "more time" for us to spend on our Money Making Skills to bring in more income!

Books are by no means the newest technology available, but they are still extremely effective. You don't have to use the latest and greatest technology to get results. Don't fall into the "new-itis" trap that was discussed earlier in this book. Writing this book, along with creating the website, is using technology so we can connect with people all around the world, whom we would have never met otherwise. The books feeds right into another New Rule: *Whoever Has the Biggest Rolodex, Wins* (chapter 10 in this book), which will help us achieve more of our goals.

The potential downside of creating time leverage is that it can end up costing you time and money if you make the wrong decision. For example, how much time leverage would we have really gained if this book only sold 20 copies. Not much. In fact, it would end up costing us time because writing the book took longer than us talking to 20 people.

Also, in the New Rule: Calculating Your ROLIFE chapter, we discussed opportunity cost. What would have been the opportunity cost on writing a book that did poorly? Fortunately, we know this book will sell way more than 20 copies!

Leverage can be a great money and time multiplier for you, but it can also go against you and cause some real problems. Make sure you evaluate all leverage opportunities carefully!

Hope For the Best, Plan For the Worst

"Hope for the best, plan for the worst" is a common saying among entrepreneurs. This saying can have many different applications to various areas of your life. However, there isn't a more appropriate time to discuss this than immediately after the section on leverage. It's very easy to get caught up in the excitement of an idea you have and think that nothing can go wrong. That lack of judgement can lead to disastrous results, especially if you're using financial leverage.

The real estate boom and bust is the first thing that comes into our minds. In the early 2000's, real estate prices just kept going higher and higher. Many people's houses doubled in value within a couple of years! Everyone was talking about how real estate was the place to be and that if you weren't buying houses, you were losing out. Some people bought houses that were more than they could afford at the time, with the idea that the value would go up in the next couple of years and they would cash in. Others borrowed money on their house and used it to buy more houses. They would then borrow money on the new house they bought and buy another house with it!

Once the real estate prices dropped, they were in major trouble because they were too leveraged. If they had simply followed the "Hope for the best, plan for the worst" philosophy, most would have been better off. If only they asked themselves, "What would happen if the prices didn't go up? Would I be able to afford the house?"

Following the "Hope for the best, plan for the worst" is much easier said than done. It's very easy to get caught up in all the excitement of something or think you have everything perfectly figured out and nothing can go wrong. If you want to become an Anti Suit Entrepreneur, you must constantly follow this philosophy. Those that can put emotion and excitement aside for a minute to evaluate both the potential positives and potential negatives of a situation will greatly reduce their chance of becoming financially ruined. By reducing your risk and protecting yourself, you greatly increase the chances of becoming financially successful.

We've seen many people get financially ruined because of a small speed bump in life. One small thing has a ripple effect and progressively causes bigger and bigger problems. We've watched many people act as though their job or their income will last forever. So they buy a house, get a new car, take vacations, and never put money aside for "what if" scenarios. What happens if that job income stops flowing in for a couple of weeks. Many people are so leveraged out that even missing one paycheck would have disastrous results. They couldn't afford their next car payment, or would have to start racking up credit card debt to get by, or take a loan out on their 401(k). These actions cause a ripple effect throughout the rest of their lives from which they often cannot recover. Those situations could have been avoided by putting money aside in an emergency fund or not buying the most expensive car you think you can afford.

Now we are not preaching from a mountain top to you on this subject. We've made our financial and life mistakes by not following the "Hope for the best, but plan for the worst" philosophy. But we learned our lessons and always looked at the possible downside of things. If something can slide uncontrollably out of control and cause major issues, we avoid it. The next chapter will cover our strategy for how you can protect yourself.

Learn the Rules and Play by Them

No matter what you do, you need take the time to learn the rules so you can play by them. Different ways of generating income have different rules associated with them. Many people never learn the rules because they are never taught in school. By rules, we mean what you can and can't do and how to maximize the income you generate. It's really amazing how much money you can generate, once you learn the rules.

Most people are taught through school and their parents that you get your paycheck and the government will take out taxes. Whatever is left over is yours to spend. If you're lucky, you'll get a tax refund after you file your taxes. That's about it, other than some vague recommendations that get passed around here and there that usually end up doing more harm than good for people's finances.

Not understanding the rules actually cost many people the opportunity of becoming an Anti Suit Entrepreneur because they think they don't have the money to get started down the path. That couldn't be farther from the truth. In fact, the U.S. Government, and many other governments, have rules set up that encourage you to become an Anti Suit Entrepreneur. Employees who get a W-2 form have the worst rules out of all the groups. The rules are very limited on what you can and cannot do.

If you own a business or get a 1099 (usually called independent contractors), you have a whole separate set of rules than an employee does. The rules allow you to deduct business expenses. A business expense is defined as an ordinary and necessary expense in order to conduct business. Pretty much in any business you start, you will need a computer. Let's say you decide to start a new business and buy a computer for $1,000. You keep the receipt and at tax time list the computer as a business expense. Now you're able to deduct that from your taxes, which means you do not have to pay taxes on the money spent! If you're in the 25% tax bracket, that means you just saved $250 (25% x $1,000)!

You're also able to deduct a part of your house or apartment as a home office. If a person is renting a house for $1,000 a month and sets up a small home office that takes up 10% of the apartment (say an extra bedroom, den or corner somewhere), you can now deduct 10% of rent and utilities as business expenses. You can also deduct traveling, mileage on your car, your cell phone, and meals out, to just name a few.

Over the years, we've read many articles by CPA's that say the average U.S. family can save $5,000 to $15,000 a year in taxes just by starting a business out of their home and learning the tax rules. That does not require them to spend more money, but just to learn the rules and to categorize current expenses as business expenses. Let's say you spend the time to learn the rules and end saving $5,000 a year in taxes. That works out to about an extra $415 a month of cash in (CI) for you. We both started our first Anti Suit Entrepreneur business venture for less than $500 a month. Learning the rules that the U.S. Government put in place, basically funded us in becoming Anti Suit Entrepreneurs. Spending a few hours learning the rules, in order to save $5,000 or more dollars a year, is a no brainer to us.

Understand that we are writing from the perspective of a U.S. Citizen. If you're in a different country, you'll have to research the rules that apply to you. We're going to avoid a lot of the lingo in order to avoid confusion. Ultimately, this is not a tax book, but is intended to expose you to new ideas and ways of thinking. Before you start applying these rules, you'll want to check with a tax professional. We have really just scratched the surface of the business tax rules. There's so much more you can deduct and do. It actually takes very little time and work on your part. The resources section of this chapter will point you in the direction of more detailed information that will take you through everything step by step.

Don't be an Idiot With Your Money

This is much easier said than done. It's easy to spend the money as fast as it comes in, often times on things that you can't remember a week later nor have an impact on your becoming an Anti Suit Entrepreneur and developing the life you want.

We speak from experience on this and are not pointing fingers. Looking back, we put a little too much into "fun" money. It was fun living in penthouses in different cities, eating out all the time, traveling on every whim, and buying way too many $16 mojitos in South Beach, Miami. Instead, we could have saved a lot of that money and used it for creating passive income.

We're not saying to be a miser with money and not to enjoy life. At the same time, don't spend all of your money and never get financially ahead. There's a happy medium between having fun and putting money toward saving and passive income. You need to find that happy medium for yourself. We're not going to tell you what to do with your money because at the end of the day, it's your money and your life.

No matter how little money you make, you need to start developing that habit of putting money aside ASAP. You don't become an Anti Suit Entrepreneur and then start acting like one. You act like one first and that will help you become one. If you don't, you'll have cash going out as fast as it's coming in. This happened to someone we used to work with. He made between $200,000 to $250,000 a year in recurring income, a very good income. However, numerous times he borrowed money from both of us to cover short term expenses. One time, he asked to borrow $600 from Chris on a Monday, so he could pay a bill and would pay Chris back on Friday when his next recurring check came in. He had to borrow money because he was an idiot with his money. It wasn't like an unexpected emergency or medical bill popped up. He just spent money on unnecessary and stupid stuff. He was just totally undisciplined with his money.

We often ask ourselves as we are spending money, "Am I being an idiot with my money?" It might not be the most politically correct way to put it, but it gets the point across, which is the most important thing. No matter how tight you are on money, start developing the habit of "not being an idiot with money" and putting money aside into a savings account. Even if you can only put $50 a month to begin, do it! Habits will either make you or break you as an Anti Suit Entrepreneur.

ANTI SUIT
CHARGE AHEAD
HOMEWORK

Get it. Read it. **Apply it.**

Register for the Anti Suit Entrepreneur Online Seminar Series, which includes a seminar on this chapter, *Why Most People Never "Get Ahead"* at our website address www.AntiSuitEntrepreneur.com/chapter3

Chapter 4

Cash is King. But, Diversified Cash Flow "Rules the Land"

What's the riskiest financial move you can make? It's relying on one source of income. Yet, almost everyone does it and never thinks twice about it! It doesn't matter if you're an employee, a business owner, or a highly paid professional. What would happen to your finances and livelihood if your job was lost, your business dropped off, or you were injured? For most people, those scenarios would have them knocking on the door of financial ruin.

Over the last 10 years from our personal experiences, watching other people both struggle and thrive, and our constantly researching and evaluating things, we've come to the conclusion that creating Diversified Cash Flow is the way to go to truly live the life you want and to protect yourself from the unexpected curve balls of life. It's not a matter of *if* life throws you a curve ball; it's a matter of *when* life throws you a curve ball. You'll get them. The question is, will you be prepared?

You have probably heard the phrase "don't put all of your eggs in one basket." You want to create different ways that cash will flow into your bank account. That's Diversified Cash Flow. That way, if one source of cash flow drops off or gets completely wiped out, you're protected because you have other sources of cash flow that are independent of each other. Diversified Cash Flow can also help out in case you get injured, have to deal with family emergencies, or if the economy tanks, assuming you have developed at least one source of income that continues to flow in when you don't work.

Can you recall what you felt in the last quarter of 2007 when it was announced that our economy was in big trouble? Was it scary to think what was coming? Some people call this time and years following it (even up to the writing of this book), the Great Recession. To be honest, when a economy turns downward, it affects everyone. It affected us. If people spend less, in one way or another, it affected all of our businesses. However, since we had Diversified Cash Flow, we were not worried at all. Contrast this to what we see in the people in our lives who hadn't developed Diversified Cash Flow.

The interesting thing, as we look back, is that since we were not worried about the economy (because of Diversified Cash Flow), it allowed us to have a "clear head" and actually see the opportunities that were available in this Great Recession. So instead of being afraid of the Great Recession, we embraced it. It allowed us to create more streams of Diversified Cash Flow.

Even if you will never become an Entrepreneur (or beyond that an Anti Suit Entrepreneur), don't allow your job (the active income source for most people) to be the only thing you have. Let the Great Recession be a lesson to you.

To demonstrate the concept of Diversified Cash Flow, look at the figure below. You can see three letters that represent the three types of cash flow discussed in the previous chapter: A = Active, R = Recurring, & P = Passive. This figure represents how the cash flows interact with each other to create Diversified Cash Flow. Active cash flow can feed into (and create) recurring and passive cash flow. Recurring can feed into (and create) passive cash flow.

The rest of this chapter will take you through the steps that we went through to create Diversified Cash Flow. We've also incorporated lessons learned over the years that we would do, if we had to do it all over again. The goal is to give you a road map for creating your own Diversified Cash Flow.

Step #1: Create Your Foundation

You need enough active income to pay the bills and have money so you can invest in creating recurring income. For most people, their active income will be from a job. If you don't currently have enough active income to pay your bills, do not start working on recurring income! Recurring income takes time and money to develop. If you're worried about paying your mortgage or rent next month, you need to put all of your focus on generating enough active income to take care of your immediate needs.

We cannot stress this enough because we've seen so many people fall into the hype and promises from websites and scam artists about how fast they can make recurring income in the next 30 days to pay the bills. It's just not true. Now, we are not saying wait until your life is perfect to start creating recurring income. We just want to make sure you don't put yourself in a very bad financial situation.

In addition to generating enough active income to pay the bills, what expenses can you cut back on? Every single person we have mentored over the years has had expenses that could be reduced. Cutting back on unnecessary expenses equates to an instant increase in your active income because you have less cash going out.

Chris started creating Diversified Cash Flow while he was in college, so it was much easier for him to reduce expenses rather than trying to create additional active income with minimum wage paying jobs around campus. He got rid of cable TV, cut back on the number of "happy hours" he went to, and stopped getting coffee out. On average, these changes saved him about $250 a month. The $250 is what he used to start creating his recurring income. By the time he graduated from Virginia Tech, he was generating enough Diversified Cash Flow that he didn't have to get a job. In fact, he was making more recurring income than what many starting jobs were paying. Years later, he appreciates *now* the Diversified Cash Flow he developed rather than having a pitcher of beer every Tuesday night at Happy Hour *then*.

Step #2: Start Working on Recurring Income

When you have enough active income to cover your basic needs and living expenses, it's time to start working on your recurring income. Just as with earning a college degree or developing a high paying career, building up recurring income does not happen overnight. It takes time, money, and commitment to develop it. It's best to start building your recurring income part time, while you're still working your job to bring in your active income. This is the most sure-fire and safest way to start building up recurring income.

This is exactly what Jason did. After deciding that he did not want to buy the law firm he was running, Jason focused his attention on creating recurring income.

Jason set up a transition plan once he made the decision that he didn't want to continue with the law firm. Part of that transition plan was for himself and part was for the new owner of the law firm. That owner needed to transition some of his staff into the position to carry on the duties in order to keep the firm profitable and Jason needed to have a schedule that allowed him to help the law firm while putting time into his recurring income.

Jason essentially had active income by transitioning out of the law firm (both for the benefit of the new owner and himself) and spent the rest of his time building his recurring income. After two years, Jason had enough recurring income from his new business that he didn't need the active income generated from the law firm. He did stay on six more months to finish the transition.

Most people never spend the time figuring out how to incorporate recurring income with their active income. Therefore, they never change their ROLIFE.

Step #3: Recurring Income > Active Income

A common mistake people make is that they quit their job too soon when they start making recurring income. It's very easy to do this because the excitement of earning recurring income can make you feel as though you're on "Cloud 9." Quitting your job too soon is also one of the top reasons why people don't create Diversified Cash Flow and never become an Anti Suit Entrepreneur.

We know a person who had over $100,000 in the bank and was making a six-figure income from his active income source.   He started working on his recurring income source and built it to about $50,000 a year income. Nice.   However, once the person got a taste of the "Cloud 9" recurring income, he mentioned to Jason and Chris that he was going to quit his job, which would cut off that six-figure active income source.   Jason and Chris both showed concern for this and this person replied, "I have plenty of money in the bank. Everything will be fine."

Two years later, this person was limping along and struggling and had to go work for someone. Sadly, we are not sure he will ever get away from the active income treadmill.

Keep working on your recurring income until it's greater than your active income and you have a six month emergency fund built up. An emergency fund is money set aside that is used only in emergencies! It's not something that is dipped into to buy a new TV, a down payment on a sports car, or take a vacation. It's there to be used when unexpected things happen, such as medical bills, a drop or loss in income, or a family emergency. Calculate it by figuring out how much money you need on a monthly basis to live. This amount includes everything that is CO (Cash Out) on a monthly basis: debt payments, mortgage or rent, car payments, food, gas, and all those other little expenses. Once you calculate your total, multiply it by six and you have the amount you need for a six month emergency fund. Every person's emergency fund will be different. Some will need to save more and some will need to save less.

We're advocates of creating an emergency fund because when you're transitioning from living off active income to living off of recurring income, unexpected things will happen! It's prudent to have an emergency fund set aside for unexpected things. Some people hear us say that and think, "Gosh, it would take me forever to save that." Not necessarily if you're not being stupid with your money. Let's say a person makes $50,000 a year in active income and is starting to generate recurring income that matches it. That's close to a $100,000 a year income! As long as the person isn't being unwise and spending all that extra money, he can set it aside and quickly build up a six month emergency fund.

Many people want to know exactly how long it will take them to build up enough recurring income to replace their active income. There's no clear cut answer on this because there are many variables that are dependent on the person: How much do you need to make? What are you doing to create the recurring income? How much time can you put into creating it? And so on... It typically takes two to five years to create your recurring income that meets or exceeds your active income. Look at those two to five years as an investment. During that time you will be developing various Money Making Skills and also creating an income source that will keep bringing in money for years, even decades to come.

Step #4: Start Diversifying Your Cash Flow

Once you have a six month emergency fund saved and your recurring income is greater than your active income, it's time to create Diversified Cash Flow. At this point, most people will quit their job or reduce the time they are putting into creating their active income. Whether you continue to work a job or not is entirely up to you. However, it's our experience that it's very difficult to create Diversified Cash Flow while working a job. Typically, working a job, you'll have very limited hours in order to research, pursue, and create Diversified Cash Flow. In fact, in many cases, continuing to work a job may actually cost you money.

Most people who have developed a full time recurring income have also developed a strong set of Money Making Skills and the Anti Suit Entrepreneur Mindset (Chapter 5), which can be used in creating Diversified Cash Flow. Once we both established our recurring income, the opportunities for creating Diversified Cash Flow were almost countless! We had so many opportunities and ideas we could pursue. We literally had to sort and pick which ones we wanted to undertake, a very good problem to have!

Over the next few years, we did everything from day trading with stocks to FX trading to setting up a small business media company to creating educational resources to help other aspiring Anti Suit Entrepreneurs, and much more! We did all of this while the recurring income we developed kept generating income on a regular basis that paid the bills. We now have a Diversified Cash Flow that has over ten different sources of income. We're not telling you this to brag, but rather show what can be accomplished when you follow the plan we have laid out in this chapter.

When you reach this point, your Diversified Cash Flow will look very different from ours because you'll have different Money Making Skills, opportunities, and interests that you want to pursue. When you do reach this point, you'll have what you need to create Diversified Cash Flow that consists of active, recurring, and passive Income. You'll truly be living the Anti Suit Entrepreneur lifestyle and dictating the terms of your LIFE.

Step #5: Focus on Bigger Things

Creating Diversified Cash Flow and becoming an Anti Suit Entrepreneur isn't just about getting a lot of digits in your bank account. It's about doing exactly what you want in life and impacting the world in some way. You'll get to the point where you won't have to worry about money, and to maintain all of this it could require just a few hours a month. This freedom opens up the door to pursue anything you want without being concerned about money.

Want to start a charity? Want to get involved in politics to make a difference? Want both you and your spouse to be full time parents? Want to take a year vacation?

Money is what makes the world go around. You don't have to like this fact or agree with it, but it's true. You need money to work on your bigger projects and aspirations. Diversified Cash Flow is your ticket to do so.

We're not going to spend much time talking about this section or telling you what you need to do. You have your own big dreams for your life or how you want to impact and change the world. Depending on what you want to do, you may need $100,000 or $10,000,000 in Diversified Cash Flow. However, if you can't take care of yourself financially, you can't take care of other people or bigger issues.

Where to Start

It can be confusing, exciting, and a bit scary as you start down your path of creating recurring income and then building that into a solid Diversified Cash Flow. Understand that while the changes in the economy are closing some doors, mostly in the area of "secure jobs," the changes are opening up numerous other doors to different ways of creating recurring income. There is really an unprecedented opportunity in this economy for any individual, regardless of background and education, to build Diversified Cash Flow.

Step #1: Cut back on unnecessary expenses. Look at your credit card and bank statements to figure out where you can cut back. Do you really need Starbucks coffee every day?

Step #2: Determine exactly how much you need to live off of each month. We won't cover the details of creating a monthly budget because there are countless free resources that already do a great job. Spend the time and figure out exactly how much you need to live on a monthly basis.

Step #3: Open up a free, no-fee checking or savings account at your bank or one of the online banks. Set up an automatic transfer of at least $300 a month into this account. Do not touch the account unless it's for creating recurring income. Even though you may not know how you'll create recurring income, you need to start setting money aside and getting into the habit of investing money each month into your financial future. This is your seed money.

Step #4: Figure out how much active income you need to cover your monthly budget from Step #2 and your monthly seed money from Step #3. Do you currently have enough active income to cover those two things? If not, look to see what expenses you can cut out further and then start looking for ways to increase it.

Step #5: Keep reading this book! We'll walk you through the rest of the New Rules so you have a solid foundation for starting your recurring income.

It goes without saying, but we'll say it anyway. Do these five steps. Don't read it, say it's great, and move on without doing anything. Set up a reminder in your smartphone or write it on your to-do list right now to start working on this tomorrow.

ANTI SUIT
CHARGE AHEAD
HOMEWORK

Get it. Read it. **Apply it.**

Register for the Anti Suit Entrepreneur Online Seminar Series, which includes a seminar on this chapter, *Cash is King; But Diversified Cash Flow Rules the Land* at www.AntiSuitEntrepreneur.com/chapter4

Chapter 5

The Anti Suit Entrepreneur Mindset: Getting Off the Roller Coaster

As you become an Anti Suit Entrepreneur, your biggest enemy is going to be you. Yes, you read that right. *You* will be your own biggest enemy. How often do you have self doubt, second guess yourself, or crush your own self esteem? Most people don't like to admit it, but everyone beats himself up and turns into his own biggest enemy.

The mindset you have will determine how you act and react under certain situations. An example of how you can be your own worst enemy is the "keeping up with the Joneses" principle. After Jason completed law school, he immediately started working on his Anti Suit Entrepreneur plan. Many people around him were consumed with fancy cars, flashing money, and just generally appearing as though they had money. This is called "keeping up with the Joneses." A bad mindset can have you worrying about what kind of car you drive, how much money it appears you make, and other superficial areas on which people spend way too much time. Jason was doing pretty well financially even while he made the transition to Anti Suit Entrepreneur, but he didn't change his plan, despite the judgement he received from some people. We know what you are thinking. "Who cares about those people?" You're right, but do you realize how many people ask that question and then turn around and worry about the opinions of others?

This is a bad mindset and can greatly impact your plan because you are worrying about what other people think. It's a disaster to worry about that stuff. Jason would not allow himself to fall prisoner to what other people thought. He did what he thought was the right thing and didn't become his own worst enemy. This is a hard thing to do. It's harder than people care to admit.

Your mindset can literally make or break you as an Anti Suit Entrepreneur or as a person. Over the years, we have seen people self destruct because they hadn't developed the Anti Suit Entrepreneur mindset.

Having an undeveloped mindset will cause the dreaded up and down emotional roller coaster, where your emotions are up one minute and then down the next. This constant up and down of emotions isn't productive, healthy, or helpful to your life, or to becoming an Anti Suit Entrepreneur. We've all been on this emotional roller coaster and know people who are absolute wrecks from the constant ups and downs of their emotions.

Stopping or getting off the emotional roller coaster is much easier said than done. It also takes time, so don't expect any overnight miracles. This chapter will take you through key points that will help you to minimize the ups and downs of the roller coaster and then to eventually get off of it altogether. Once you're finished with the constant ups and downs, you'll be a happier person with less stress and more success. These points are exactly what we focus on every day and, when needed, remind each other of them. They are also what we teach and focus on with people with whom we have mentor style relationships.

Life is Too Short

Is it faster to travel on a flat road or a road that constantly goes up and down like a roller coaster? Obviously, it's much faster and easier to travel on a flat road because you're not wasting energy and time on going up and down. You can go into cruise control on a flat road.

With that in mind, you'll get more done and go more places in life if you travel on a flat road rather than on the emotional roller coaster. If you don't develop your mindset, you're going to achieve a lot less because of your ups and downs, just like a car going fewer miles on a tank of gas when driving through the mountains. Developing your Anti Suit Entrepreneur mindset will help you spend more of your life on the flat road and less time on the roller coaster.

People often are amazed at how much we get done and how efficient we are in our various businesses. We used to think that resulted from the various productivity techniques we developed over the years. But after teaching those techniques to other people, we still saw that people were having issues. That's when we realized how important our Anti Suit Mindset was in helping us get things done.

Since we are not constantly on the ups and downs of the emotional roller coaster, we're getting more done. Once we started helping people develop their mindset, while implementing our productivity techniques, they started getting a lot more accomplished, just as we were. The benefits of the Anti Suit Entrepreneur mindset went beyond productivity gains. People saw increases in their Diversified Cash Flow, their Money Making Skills, their rolodex, and achievement of their goals. Basically, they saw increases across the board.

The increases boiled down to the fact they were spending less time on an emotional roller coaster and more time on the flat road. The bottom line is that life is too short to squander it on an emotional roller coaster. There's too much to get done!

Action Always Beats Perfection. Always.

Taking action and "just doing it" always beats waiting and planning for perfection. This statement is especially true if you're brand new. If you're brand new to something, you don't know what you don't know. Since you know very little on the subject, it's nearly impossible to lay out a perfect plan.

We've seen many people over the years, who want to make the transition to becoming an Anti Suit Entrepreneur, get stuck in planning purgatory while they try to figure out every single detail and step of the process. We've watched people spend years stuck in planning purgatory because they are trying to lay out a perfect plan in something they know next to nothing about. They are trying to plan for every "what if" scenario for the next five years. Planning for all the "what if" scenarios is impossible! It would be like a person who wants to be an Olympic swimmer, who spends all of his time watching videos and reading books, but never jumps into the pool to start swimming laps because he is afraid of flopping around a bit in the water.

When we started becoming Anti Suit Entrepreneurs, we knew some people who were creating the perfect plan for themselves. Years later, after we had achieved our success, those people were still stuck in planning purgatory! Did we have the perfect plan or know all the pieces of the puzzle to becoming an Anti Suit Entrepreneur? No, we didn't. In fact, there were a lot more unknowns than knowns to us when we started. The difference for us was that we made a very basic plan and then took action (and lots of it).

That mindset of taking action is what allowed us to have success. We're convinced that **action will always beat perfection**. Now, we're not saying to take blind action without a basic plan in place. Most people err on the side of getting stuck in planning purgatory rather than taking blind action.

People get stuck in planning purgatory, typically, for three reasons:

▸ They haven't developed an action oriented mindset.
▸ They have an excuse or a reason as to why they really don't want to accomplish what they are working on.
▸ They are afraid of failing.

If you haven't developed your mindset yet, that's fine. This concept and others that follow, will help you do that. It's impossible for us, through this book, to help you with an excuse or reason as to why you're not doing something. You either need to work with a mentor to get past that excuse or obstacle or move onto something else.

Now, if you're afraid or embarrassed of failing, you need to get over that. That's exactly what the next section discusses...

Get Used to Failing. A Lot!

This may sound odd, but you need to get used to failing a lot. Many people are afraid or embarrassed about failing. However, the most successful people in life, fail the most. Did you learn how to ride a bike without falling off and skinning your knees? Probably not.

Something weird happens as we get older. We are sure you have heard people say how uninhibited we were as children. We all were. When you're young, you just want to have fun. You don't care what people think if you fail. Then society brainwashes us and makes us worry about failing. You have to lose to win. You need bad times to have good times. You have to fail to succeed. It's really common sense when you think about it.

Did we fail a lot on our journey of becoming Anti Suit Entrepreneurs? You bet we did. Actually, we still fail a lot today as we're pursuing new opportunities. The word fail has almost become a bad word in the English language. In turn, that's caused a lot of people to avoid trying something or pursuing a goal because they are afraid or embarrassed about failing.

Rather than being embarrassed or afraid of failing, you should embrace it. It's the Failing Forward concept. This quote from Thomas Edison sums up the Failing Forward concept, "I have not failed. I've just found 10,000 ways that won't work." Every time you fail, you learn something new and you've moved closer to your goal. Here's our approach to Failing Forward:

Step #1: Take action - Avoid planning purgatory.

Step #2: Fail - You're going to fall off the bike.

Step #3: Evaluate - What went wrong? What could have been done differently?

Step #4: Take action - Get back on the bike and work toward your goal.

It's important to evaluate and reflect upon your failure. This is how you learn and make sure that you do not repeat that failure. You need to accept that failing is part of becoming successful, but repeating the same failures over and over is just stupid and nonproductive.

The More You Fail, The More You Succeed

It's not only important to get used to failing, but to also realize that the more you fail, the faster you will succeed. You want to develop the mindset of quickly evaluating your most recent failure and then getting up, brushing yourself off, and getting back to taking action toward your goal. As you're developing your Anti Suit Entrepreneur mindset, you'll probably get back on the emotional roller coaster after you fail at something. The quicker you can get off the emotional roller coaster, the better.

You can't get into a mental funk every time you fail. To help you develop the right mindset, you need to develop the opposite of a mental funk, which is acknowledging to yourself that you failed and that you're closer to your goal now. Every time we "fail forward," we remind ourselves that we moved a little bit closer toward our goal.

Thomas Edison has another quote that is appropriate for this section, "Many of life's failures are people who did not realize how close they were to success when they gave up." Isn't it quite interesting how Edison has multiple quotes around failing, yet he's one of the most successful inventors of all time? Edison's quote should tell you something about the importance of changing your mindset about failing. It should also drive home the point of how you shouldn't be embarrassed about failing.

One of the reasons we're successful is because we fail a lot, evaluate, make adjustments, and get back to taking action on our goals **quickly**. We hardly spend any time on the emotional roller coaster because we've developed the Anti Suit Entrepreneur mindset. Simply put, we don't let our failures slow us down. Many people don't talk about failing, but we've noticed similar traits in other successful people. Develop the mindset that, as you fail, you're still moving toward your goal and you need to get back into taking action.

Stop the Self Destructive Self Talk. Now.

Does your mind ever seem like a battleground where part of it is telling you that you can do something and another part of it is saying you're a failure or not cut out for it and are just wasting time? That's called Self Talk. There are two types: Constructive Self Talk and Destructive Self Talk. They remind us of how childhood cartoons have an angel and devil standing on a person's opposite shoulders, with both of them whispering what the person should do.

The words you speak out loud to someone and speak to yourself lay the foundation for your Self Talk. Self Talk is learned behavior from years of choosing good words or bad words. As with any behavior or habit, you have the ability to change it. You start changing Destructive Self Talk to Constructive Self Talk one word at a time. Let's talk about some of the most destructive words you can use and how to go about changing them.

If is only two letters, but they are a very destructive set of letters. *If* is destructive because it's a weak word that shows uncertainty. Compare, "*If* I become an Anti Suit Entrepreneur and can stop working for my mean boss" to "*When* I become an Anti Suit Entrepreneur, I can stop working for my mean boss." The statement using *if* is showing uncertainty about your future and has an "it may or may not happen" attitude to it. On the other hand, the statement using *when* is assuming that it will happen in the future. *When* is a powerful word that shows certainty about you creating the future you want.

Another destructive word is *cannot* or *can't*. By using one of these words, you are setting yourself up for failure before you even begin. A common use of *cannot* is when it comes to purchasing something. People often say, "I can't afford that..." Replace that Destructive Self Talk with, "How can I afford that?" It's a subtle but powerful difference. Using *can* and *how* is acknowledging that you don't have the money at the moment, but are framing your mindset into the fact that you have control and the power to afford it. You just need to figure out how you can.

Most people use *if* and *cannot* dozens of times a day without even realizing it. Using these words has a ripple effect in your daily activities, your long term mindset, and, eventually, your results (or lack of results) on a long-term basis.

Think of using Destructive Self Talk as if you're eating junk food. Eating that cupcake today isn't going to make you fat or diabetic today. However, eating a cupcake every day, along with other junk food daily, day after day over the years, has a very destructive impact on your health.

The first step is to start becoming aware of what Destructive Self Talk you're using and how often you're doing it. *If* and *cannot* are the two most common. You, like everyone else, have other words or phrases you're using. Once you start becoming aware of the words, then it's time to start changing them to Constructive Self Talk. Changing a few little words will have a big impact on your future.

Stop Caring What Others Think

No matter what you do in life, you'll think people are criticizing you, making fun of you, or thinking that you're an idiot. Guess what? Most of that is in your mind. Trust us, people are too worried about themselves to spend more than a few seconds thinking of or criticizing you. Most of the time no one is even thinking of you. You're just imagining them thinking of you!

Everything we described above about Self Talk (that you were probably nodding your head to) is exactly what's going on with other people. They are too worried about themselves to worry about you! Besides, most people are genuinely nice people, who don't care too much about what you're doing, but want you to do well.

There is a small percentage of people who will criticize you. You will need to develop thick skin so you don't let them bother you. Some of those people are just jerks. You have to learn to ignore the jerks out there because no matter what you do, there will be jerks around. If you actually develop a mindset and grow confident in yourself, there will be a lot fewer of them around you. Jerks seem to prey on people who are insecure with themselves.

You will have some friends and family members criticize and judge you. More often than not, that's because they are jealous of you going after your dreams. The phrase "misery loves company" is appropriate for these situations. You going after your dreams or trying to improve your life will remind some people about their failed dreams or the life of mediocrity into which they have fallen. This realization causes some people to get mad at themselves and then lash out at you with criticisms or rude comments. If you fail and don't achieve your dreams, in a twisted way, it makes the person feel better and less like a failure. But, if you achieve your goals or improve your life, it just reminds that person even more about his own failures or lack of effort he has put into life.

You can try to change these people or argue with them, but that's usually a waste of time. Generally, it's best to just ignore their comments and avoid the person. You're seeing the person's true colors. Do you really want to be around someone like that? Depending on the person and your relationship, you may not be able to cut the person out. In that scenario, it's best to just not bring up what you're up to, grow thick skin, and keep moving forward toward your goal.

Jason received quite a few criticisms and odd looks from people when he started down the road of becoming an Anti Suit Entrepreneur. His peers and fellow law school students even thought he was crazy that he wasn't buying the law firm and putting his law degree to use by becoming a lawyer. Why? Jason still doesn't know for sure, but looking back on it, it was most likely because his decision threatened everything for which they worked. Think about it. In law school, his first-year class was over 120 people and when they graduated, there were around 30. Those 30 or so people had given up their lives for four years, some were divorced over it, some spent less time with their kids, and many were passed over for promotions and other things, because they were so busy with law school. After all that sacrifice, law school had to be worth it. Right? Jason's decision to go a different direction was like a confirmation of their mistake. Although Jason doesn't regret going to law school, it was clear that many of his classmates sure regretted it.

Jason simply was trying to avoid a life full of stress, kissing judges' asses, and working long days. It made many people face the "ugly" side of their career path and therefore criticize Jason.

Jason has thick skin and kept focused on his goal of becoming an Anti Suit Entrepreneur. He didn't let his classmates affect his goal.

He is glad he did because many of those same people today are unhealthy, work unfulfilling jobs, and look 10 years older than they really are because of all the stress.

Think Long Term. Success Doesn't Happen Over Night.

People know success doesn't happen overnight, but it seems a lot of people forget it when they are on the emotional roller coaster. What we've seen happen time and time again is that someone will be at the low point on the emotional roller coaster, get frustrated, and want to quit whatever they're doing. This decision is especially true when people are starting their journey to become an Anti Suit Entrepreneur. They know it's going to take a few years at the minimum, but when they hit a few rough patches or someone questions what they are doing, they start second guessing themselves. We've seen that second guessing lead to people pulling back and eventually quitting. We said quitting, not failing, because the person gives up on himself and stops trying.

You need to put what you're doing into perspective and constantly remind yourself of your goals! When Chris started, he was working on a four year undergraduate degree. Whenever he got frustrated (and on the emotional roller coaster) at becoming an Anti Suit Entrepreneur, he put things into perspective by looking at the time and money he was putting into a four year college degree and comparing that to where he was in his Anti Suit Entrepreneur goal. When he did this, it made him realize how much money and time he was willing to invest into a college degree and, in contrast, how little he had invested into becoming an Anti Suit Entrepreneur! These reminders helped him get off the emotional roller coaster and back to taking action.

Another way to help think long term is look back at how much you've achieved. It's easy to get so focused on your goals and moving forward, that you don't take a minute to look back at how far you've traveled. You have to look beyond how much money you've made and spent. Reflect on the Money Making Skills that you've developed, the new connections with successful people that you've made, how much your mindset has developed, and on other positive achievements. Developing these and other areas will lead to generating more money and eventually building a solid Diversified Cash Flow.

Consistency in Your Efforts

Taking consistent action and putting in consistent efforts toward your goal are important pieces to the Anti Suit Entrepreneur. Believe it or not, consistent action is actually the best way to get off the emotional roller coaster. The best way to explain this is when you're trying to get back into a workout routine or back into shape. It can be very hard to muster the motivation and energy to go to the gym and work out. Trying to get back into a five day workout routine can be overwhelming. When you do even a little bit of exercise, though, it makes everything easier. You feel better, have more energy, and are more optimistic. That little bit of exercise can even be just walking the dog or something to get the body moving.

The same idea applies to becoming an Anti Suit Entrepreneur. Taking any action will help you get off the emotional roller coaster because it'll get you refocused. Taking consistent action will help you stay off the roller coaster. Once you're in the habit of taking action, you build up momentum, and it's easier to keep that momentum going.

Being consistent and doing a little bit of work each day will produce more results and bring you closer to your goal than doing a lot of work one week and then taking the next off. Each day may not seem as though you're accomplishing a lot, but it pays off. We promise. Make sure you're taking consistent, preferably daily, action toward your goal. Results will follow.

Face the Skeletons in the Closet

We all have "skeletons in the closet" that come out and knock us off course and cause havoc in our lives. We all have different "skeletons" because different things throughout life cause them. But we all have them. "Skeletons in the closet" is the phrase that we coined for when something is triggered in you to create self imposed obstacles that slow you down or stop you from achieving your goal. These pop out at the worst times!

Earlier in this book, we shared the story of Chris having fluid in his ears and subsequent speech issues. Chris would have a "skeleton" from his closet pop out if someone made a comment about how he talked or asked him to repeat himself. These people were not poking fun or even insinuating that Chris spoke poorly. However, since Chris had issues when he was a kid, these comments would sometimes trigger the "skeleton" to come out and really screw with his self-confidence. It caused emotional roller coaster cycles of "Can I really do this? Maybe I'm not cut out for this stuff? Maybe I should do something else where I don't have to talk very much?" and some other very ugly language. It slowed Chris down, big time.

It seems that everyone has these "skeletons." Some people have more than others and some have bigger ones than others. That's just how life is and it's not fair. But the point is that everyone has them. You need to learn how to deal with your "skeletons." Dealing with them is much easier said than done.

The first thing to do is to start identifying your "skeletons" and determining what triggers them to come out.

Do the best you can to self-analyze what caused them and figure out how to deal with them. This analysis isn't an easy thing to do, but you have to confront those "skeletons" so they don't keep coming out and preventing you from having success in life.

Sometimes the way people get help with their self-analysis is through personal development courses or seminars. Some are good and some are bad. Buyer beware on these things. Just be careful to not get sucked into those incredibly expensive personal development seminars or coaching programs. From our perspective, they can do more harm than good. The bottom line is that you need to learn how to confront your own "skeletons" without having to rely on personal development courses or seminars all the time.

Developing your mindset is a never ending process. You never arrive at the "top of the mountain" because there is always room for improvement. We encourage you to come back and reread this chapter from time to time. As you develop your mindset, different topics will jump out at you or help you in the next step of your mindset development. Just as we said you should take consistent action to reach your goals, you should also consistently develop your mindset as well.

ANTI SUIT
CHARGE AHEAD
HOMEWORK

Get it. Read it. **Apply it.**

Fight the biggest enemy to your Anti Suit Entrepreneur journey: You. Proper mindset in your daily activities is critical to your success. Get a checklist that you can review on a daily basis to keep you on track. Download the Anti Suit Entrepreneur Mindset Check List at www.AntiSuitEntrepreneur.com/chapter5

Chapter 6

The Vague Recommendation: "Get a Mentor"

What sports team does not have a coach? It would be ridiculous to think of a team not having one. It is a fundamental understanding that a team needs a coach. Just as every sports team needs a coach, you need a mentor to teach you skills, help you practice those skills, and keep you accountable to your goals for yourself and the team.

We've never met a person who was successful at anything who can't give some credit to someone who helped them "learn the ropes." In fact, many successful people we have met over the years attributed their success to multiple mentors as opposed to just one person. If you have read any books in the area of entrepreneurship, business, self-help, or any other non-fiction book that is teaching related subjects, then we are not telling you anything you haven't heard before.

We wouldn't be where we are today without mentors over the years. We're not going to spend this chapter telling you why you need a mentor because the majority of people with whom we have ever talked, agrees about the need for a mentor.

The bottom line is that in order to become an Anti Suit Entrepreneur, you need a mentor or mentors. Period. You need a mentor in any area in which you want to be successful!

This chapter is going to focus on understanding the different types of mentors available, gaining the knowledge you need to find the *right* mentor for you, and avoiding the many pitfalls and scams of finding a mentor. The "Get a mentor" advice we received from books, seminars, courses, and people was very vague to us, as it is to most. The chapter will focus on those areas because many people we meet either don't have a mentor or they don't have the *right* mentor for their situation. If you're tired of the vague advice of "get a mentor," then this chapter is for you.

Three Types of Mentorship Relationships

We narrowed down the different types of mentors into three categories or types to give you more insight and direction than anyone gave us.

Type #1: Teacher Relationship

This type is often times an informal relationship where you can learn from someone successful. It could be someone you follow and learn from through their website, YouTube videos, conference calls, or video courses. It could also be someone with whom you develop a relationship (family friend, local business person, etc) and from whom you are able to learn.

You can learn a lot from this type, but it's usually not enough, because you can't ask questions or get the level of help that you need. The reality is that the mentor will share information because he enjoys teaching and helping other people, but his top priority will remain his own business and life (as it should!).

For example, we love sharing our knowledge to help people on our various websites, YouTube channels, and eCourses that we've created. We try our best to answer every email and comment that comes through, but our time is limited and it can be very hard to give in-depth answers over email.

Use this style of mentorship because it's a building block in your success, but don't rely on it as your main or only type of mentorship. That said, if you are lucky enough to have this type of relationship, and it gives you a lot of value, don't take it for granted and make sure in some way you try to repay the person who is mentoring, whether he's a personal friend or someone you follow on the Internet.

Type #2: Consultant Relationship

This type is a mentorship where you pay someone for his expertise. The relationship can vary from a one time consultation, a package deal that covers a few weeks, the completion of a project, or even a long term contract. This style guarantees you the time and attention of the person who is mentoring you because he is being compensated for his time.

For example, we had a consultant whom we paid $500 a month to keep him on retainer for when we had a specific marketing issue with which we needed help. At that time, he was worth every penny of his fee.

People spend tens of thousands of dollars on higher education (often with no real personal attention from professors). Doesn't it make sense to invest in help in specific areas when you need it? The best part is that you will probably spend less than a college degree costs and potentially make more money.

While this type of mentorship can be very valuable, make sure you're not hiring a person who has never had success in the field, but rather makes all of his money from consulting. This determination can be hard to make sometimes, but ask the questions you need to and try your best to figure it out. Also make sure that this type of mentor doesn't start taking you for granted, if you're on a long term contract with him. It's easy for a consultant to start neglecting you or taking you for granted. If you see that happening, then say something. If things don't improve, stop paying him, and move onto someone else.

Type #3: Vested Relationship

In this relationship, the mentor has a financial interest in your success. Typically you don't pay the mentor any fees or money up front, but he has a financial stake in the business or project. This style is the most powerful and financially rewarding for both the mentor and you. Since the vested mentor has a financial stake in what you're doing, the more successful you are, the more successful he is. It's as though he owns stock in your level of success and the more successful you become, the higher his stock goes. Where the consultant mentor gets paid whether you're successful or not, your vested mentor's financial interest causes him to go the extra mile in helping you achieve your goals.

We have had this style of mentorship with many people and we go the extra mile for them on a regular basis, everything from traveling to their location, working on marketing, getting up early to work on projects, or even just lying in bed with ideas bouncing around our minds about how they can have more success. We've been known to call our people very early in the morning to wake them up and say, "Last night I had this great idea... You could CRUSH IT if you did XYZ...." No one has minded those type of wake up calls!

The vested relationship style is becoming very prominent these days for a variety of reasons.

To highlight a few main reasons:

▸ Many successful people have more business than they can handle, but have a hard time finding good people with whom to work. Yes, we know this sounds crazy, but we're speaking from experience.

▸ It allows newbies to access great mentors and information when they wouldn't be able to otherwise. In a sense, it's part of the *The New College Degree.*

▸ It can lead to new sources of income and opportunities for you and the vested mentor. When Chris started down his path of becoming an Anti Suit Entrepreneur, Jason was actually his vested mentor. That initial relationship increased both of our incomes. Eventually, we became business partners in other businesses and investments. Our joint venture turned out to be very profitable.

▸ It can minimize the worry the mentor has of training his future competition because it's structured to be a win-win scenario for both parties. In fact, we've seen people make more money than their vested mentor sometimes! Other than a little bit of competitiveness in the vested mentor's ego, he's more than happy for his student's success because he's still benefitting from it financially.

There Are Two Types of Mentors

There are two types of mentors: those that have experience and success and those that do *not* have any experience and success. You want a mentor who has experience and at least some success. Most people say, "Well yea... that's common sense..." Yet once they start talking with someone, this common sense goes out the window. We're giving you a heads up on this because it's happened to people that we've mentored and to us. It's very easy to get caught up in the moment and jump into a relationship or to put an expensive coaching program on your credit card without taking time to evaluate it.

Once Chris decided to become an Anti Suit Entrepreneur, he wanted to learn as much as possible and immerse himself into entrepreneurship. While he was an undergraduate student at Virginia Tech University, he went to an informational session on a Minor in Entrepreneurship through the business college. Chris was excited to go because he wanted to learn more about entrepreneurship, build relationships with local entrepreneurs, and, hopefully, even find a mentor.

At the information session, Chris learned that one professor would be teaching the classes. Chris asked one simple question, "What's your personal experience with entrepreneurship and starting and running businesses?"

The professor replied, "I have none. I'm too risk adverse to start or invest in a business. I've been a professor for the last 25 years and have a strong interest in studying it." Chris's jaw almost dropped to the desk! At the time, without realizing it, Chris did a ROLIFE analysis. That one answer gave Chris all the information that he needed to know because he knew there would be little return on the money and time invested in getting a Minor in Entrepreneurship from someone with no practical experience. Chris was very appreciative of the professor being up front and honest about his lack of experience, but he was not the person from whom to learn entrepreneurship.

As you meet prospective mentors, always ask questions to gauge how much, if any, experience and success they have.

Beware of the Wrong Mentor

There are many people who are willing to mentor you. However, make sure that they are the "real deal" in regards to their levels of experience and success in their field.

A perfect example is a story of someone offering to be a consultant mentor to Jason. Jason was about three years into his Anti Suit Entrepreneur journey and was doing very well financially. A major coaching company (we won't mention the name out of privacy and respect) called and a coach asked Jason if he was interested in some coaching. Jason said "no" because he already had the connections for what he needed at the moment. The gentleman proceeded to get "pushy" with Jason on why Jason needed his coaching. He told Jason how he was going to fail without the coaching help that was being offered, and that he really needed to reconsider.

First of all, this coach needs to learn a little about sales. Second, telling Jason he is going to fail if he doesn't use their services is appalling to say the least. If anyone ever says you cannot or will not have success unless you work with them, buy their product, or attend their seminar, you need to immediately cut ties with that person or company.

So, because of the "pushy" attitude, Jason decided to "take the gloves off" and asked him: "What have you been successful with in entrepreneurship? Please describe to me the projects you have done and how you have accomplished them."

There was silence on the phone. After about 10 seconds, the guy fumbled with an answer that really didn't answer the question, and Jason said "You haven't done anything, have you? So you want to coach me when you haven't accomplished anything?" The prospective coach hung up on Jason.

Now we are not advocating that you drill people before you decide whether or not you want to work with them because the good people will not put up with it. However, when your gut is telling you that something is up, politely tell the person that you are fine, and then continue your search.

Another red flag is if they immediately try to sell you a $10,000 (or some other outrageously priced) mentorship package, RUN. Over the years, we have worked with people who have told us some horror stories.

There is one particular consultant mentoring program that several people have told us about. It's a stock trading mentoring program where you attend a free seminar and they pump you up and then try to sell you a $20,000+ program. To help people afford this program, they tell you to call your credit card companies to increase your line of credit so you can max them out. They even go as far as suggesting you take money out of your 401(k), IRA, or other retirement accounts in order to buy the program!

The sales people and presenters at the seminar are masters at making people feel as though this stock trading program is the only way they can learn stock trading and become successful. A person we know attended this seminar and came back on an emotional roller coaster and tied up in knots over what to do. He really wanted to learn stock trading so he could quit his job, but didn't have the cash on hand to invest $20,000+ into this program. He did know, though, with the help of the seminar instructors, that he could afford it, if he maxed out all of his credit cards and emptied his savings account. He was considering this option.

Fortunately, before he did, he talked with us. The first question we asked him was, "Let's say you go through with this program. If your credit cards are maxed out and you have no cash to invest into the stock market, where are you going to get the money with which to trade stocks?"

That stumped him, but in a good way. It helped to bring him out of the emotional excitement from the seminar and look at his situation from a more logical view point. At the time, we had a couple of mentors who were successful in stock and FX trading. We told our friend to buy a few books and courses that our mentors had recommended to us. They amounted to a few hundred dollars altogether. Once he read them, he told us, "This is exactly the stuff they were going to teach me in the stock trading program! I'm so glad I didn't spend all that money on the program."

Does that mean you should never spend $20,000 on a consultant mentoring program. No, not necessarily. Some big ticket programs out there might be worth that investment. However, if you're having to max out your credit cards or cash in your retirement, then you should not purchase it.

Know Who Will Be Mentoring You

Another point to remember from our friend's stock trading program experience is that you need to know who will actually be mentoring you. Who will be working with you? In the case of the stock trading program (and many consultant mentoring programs like it) the people presenting and selling you the mentoring are not actually the people who will be working with you. The stock trading program wanted our friend to pony up $20,000 to work with a mentor whom he never met or spoken with.

If a prospective mentor is not willing to spend time with you to answer your questions and get to know you, then that is another red flag. You need to make sure that you like and are comfortable with the mentor. You also want to make sure that he has experience and success in the field.

We've each had all three types of mentors (teacher, consultant and vested) and we've always learned the most from the people we had a relationship with and had our expectations clearly laid out before we began. You don't want to start a mentor relationship thinking one thing and the mentor thinking something else. Getting on the same page and setting expectations from the beginning is the way to go.

We understand that if a person is seeking us out as consultant or vested mentors, he is going to ask some questions before making that commitment, which is completely understandable. So we always meet with people who want us to mentor them before we begin any relationship; we need to make sure it'll work out for all of us!

Sometimes things can look perfect on paper, but, for a variety of reasons, not work out.

So, if we value our time and we are willing to do that and others aren't, then that is why we would be concerned about that potential mentorship relationship. It's like anything else. If your gut is telling you that this mentor isn't right for you, then listen to your gut. Usually when a mentor doesn't spend time and build a relationship, you need to beware. The reason is that a mentor should want to get to know you initially before he accepts you in that relationship. Regardless of whether people are paying us in a consultant role or in a vested mentorship, if we don't make sure it's someone we want to mentor, in the long-term, we'll be sorry we agreed to that role, because the money or future money (in the case of vested mentorship) is never worth it.

Your Mentor's Mentor

It is not an all or nothing level of experience and success. We all want to learn from the number one person in the field or industry. But the reality is that it is not possible to always get the top person because that person is busy or has little interest in mentoring a newbie. Which is fine. Understand that many people who are offering to mentor you may be qualified and are "on their way to entrepreneurial success."

Look at experience and success as a sliding scale from zero to ten, with zero being a newbie and ten being the highest. Does your potential mentor have *some* experience or *more* experience than you? If the answer is yes, there's potential that you could learn a lot from him. If you're at zero experience, than you can learn a lot from a mentor who's at a level two or three!

Often times it's much easier to get access to a mentor with some experience at level two, three, four or five than it is to get a mentor who is at eight, nine, or ten on the sliding scale. We've seen some people get discouraged because they cannot get personally mentored by a "ten" and then be rude or blow off a potential mentor who is a "three."

We just shake our heads in disbelief because the person is ruining a potential relationship with the "three" mentor and all of his contacts and mentors. Guess what? That "three" mentor has more experience than you and got to a "three" by doing quite a few things right. More often than not, that "three" will have a "seven" or higher level mentor to whom you could potentially be introduced or even work with. If your potential mentor is connected to another mentor who has achieved entrepreneurial success or is high up on the sliding scale, then you have the potential for creating a very powerful mentorship situation.

We're sharing this advice because it's easy to be caught up in the moment or have an overinflated ego and ruin great opportunities before they begin. No matter how successful you are in your current field, if it's outside of entrepreneurship and business, then you're most likely starting at or near "zero." That is fine; that's where we started!

Don't Be Entitled

Understand that anyone who mentors you is doing you a favor. It amazes us at times how entitled people can become. It's a first world problem. We have it so good in first world countries that we are prone to take things for granted (at least that's the excuse we make for them.)

You're not doing your mentor a favor. We've seen many people start working with a mentor and have an entitlement attitude of "He's already successful... he should help me out... or do this..." GET REAL! The mentor doesn't need you. You need the mentor. We think the best way to avoid the mistake of being perceived as entitled to your mentor is to cover some of the things you should do with your mentor.

First, never expect your mentor to show you everything he knows immediately. It's not his job to spend eight hours a day teaching you and holding your hand.

Second, never think that a mentor should invest money in you. There has to be an equal exchange between people or resentment will build. It's amazing to us how many times people have asked us to do lunch or dinner in order to pick our brains and then not pay the bill. Proper etiquette says that when you invite someone to lunch or dinner, you pay. Beyond that, when a mentor gives you his time, show some appreciation. It goes a long way.

Third, when a mentor asks you to do something, then make sure you get it done. If you consistently don't get things done, are always missing deadlines, not being on time for meetings, or always having something coming up with excuses attached to it, then that mentor isn't going to waste his time with you. Understand that even good consultant mentors (no matter how much you're paying them) will move on because they want to work with people who are serious and get things done.

Finally (and this should go without saying), if you say you're going to do something and you don't do it, that shows a crack in integrity and excuses don't change that. There are completely unexpected circumstances in unique situations, such as health problems with you or someone close to you, but generally people not doing what they say shows a lack of integrity. Period. We've actually had people bring this attitude to us after we've started to mentor them. We give people the benefit of the doubt for a while. But if those people don't change their attitude or perspective, we quickly end the relationship.

Multiple Mentors

As we grow, learn, and focus on new areas, we have found that you need new mentors, because you will begin to learn, expand, and want to experience new things. Over the years, we realized that you'll have many intended and unintended mentors and that you can always learn at least one "nugget of information."

In college, Jason worked for a major supermarket chain and a solid mentor was his store manager. This man led by example, didn't open his mouth a lot, held a balanced sense of humor with the people he managed, and was generally liked in the store. The store performed well and a big part of it was because he trusted people to take care of things in the store. If you proved yourself, he was willing to give you the responsibility if you wanted it. If something went wrong, he would back you up and wouldn't hide in the shadows. What Jason learned from him was that leadership could be achieved by quiet confidence. You didn't lead people because you have a title. You lead people by gaining their respect.

When Jason went to work for his family's law firm after business school, his dad assigned him to the lead paralegal (who was a license away from being a brilliant lawyer). The law firm focused on a very complex system based on the California Labor Code. The Labor Code had "Bible-thin" pages and measured three and one half inches thick. This guy would say "I think there is a code that addresses this..." and open the book and flip to the page (as though he was wasn't quite sure he was right) that was relevant and always land on the exact code. Jason learned from him that knowledge was power. Because of this, Jason, as a paralegal and law student, often got the better of defense lawyers with years of experience in that area of law because his knowledge of the code was so far beyond his peers.

In one of his entrepreneurial projects, Jason had a vested mentor who was fairly new himself to this type of project. The vested mentor ended up being successful because he just was too stubborn to let anyone or anything get in his way. He was a "make-it-happen" guy. Jason had always been a "make-it-happen" type of a guy, but his vested mentor gave Jason a completely different perspective on that philosophy. Jason learned that persistence and a "make-it-happen" attitude would always lead to success, even if that meant "walking through a few walls" while more skillful people used the doors. Regardless, he would always get to the next "room of success." That tenacity plays a big part in entrepreneurial success and in some ways is more important than knowing what to do.

Jason knew another person who was the ultimate sales guy. He was one of those guys that could sell ice to Eskimos! However, he would often overpromise and underdeliver on what he sold. He would say anything he needed to say in order to make the sale, which Jason did not like or respect. Jason was not even a fan of this guy at the time, but as life goes, sometimes the people you least expect are your teachers. However, Jason improved his communication Money Making Skill set by observing this person. Jason learned from observing both the man's good and bad traits.

Jason's parents were great mentors in many ways. His dad was the ultimate "nice guy" lawyer who literally built his business by making his clients feel as though they were his only client; they felt "taken care of." He could do or say almost anything to them and throw out shameless self-promotion because they liked him. He was also an excellent negotiator. Jason can remember as a kid sitting on the couch while his dad was on the phone negotiating with the other side on his client's cases. Jason didn't quite know what was going on or understand what he was doing, but Jason understood the concept of negotiating; Jason learned and absorbed a lot from his father's mentoring.

Jason's mom was a quiet leader and was in many ways the "glue" that held his parents' business together. She is extremely organized, very detail oriented, and nothing got past her. She was often the "buffer" between his dad and the staff when tensions ran high in that stressful law practice. Jason learned those organizational skills, attention to detail, and how to be a "buffer" between people to keep the peace during stressful times.

Remember that you're going to have many intended and unintended mentors over the years and that you can learn a "nugget of knowledge" from all of them. Sometimes that "nugget of knowledge" is learning how *not* to do things, which can be just as valuable as learning how to.

They're Not Gods. They're Not Perfect.

No one is perfect in this world and neither are your mentors. It's common for a person to put his mentor on a pedestal and potentially overlook any character or personal flaws. So don't get caught up in thinking that your mentor is an amazing person in every aspect of his life. We fell into this trap and don't want you to.

We had a mentor who was one of the top people in the entire industry. People would find out that he was mentoring us and grow instantly jealous. We learned a lot from this person, but we put him up on a pedestal and overlooked certain flaws, until, he did something in his personal life that crossed our line in the sand when it came to personal ethics. We ended the relationship with him very quickly after we learned what he did.

What he did in his personal life was just foreshadowing to what he was about to do in our industry and the business world. He ended up financially hurting a company with which we got him connected and also many groups of people. Everything he did was legal, but it was in the ethical and moral grey area. We were guilty by association in many people's eyes and had our reputations dinged and lost business over it.

We were upset and furious over what had happened and at what he did and, also, at ourselves for overlooking personal character flaws because he was such a brilliant person in our industry. Now, we have a rule where we won't do business with people who are unethical in any areas of their lives. It's our belief that if you're unethical in your personal life, then you are or will become unethical in the business world. We want nothing to do with that because it always ends costing more in the long run.

Respect your mentors, learn from them, but don't put them on pedestals and overlook their flaws. Often times you're not going to really know if your mentor is an ethical or unethical person when you start working with him. Don't get in the mindset that you need to hook them up to a lie detector test or take them to confession at a church before you start working them though! Do what we do: learn as much as possible from them, but keep your eyes and ears open so you don't overlook unethical flaws.

Over the years, you will have great, good, and bad mentors. Learn as much as possible from each person because it'll help you become a better Anti Suit Entrepreneur, but don't become a "labrador follower" and do exactly what they do. We've seen some people become so enamored with their mentors that they have success, but don't stay true to themselves. Remember, becoming an Anti Suit Entrepreneur is about living life on your terms, not someone else's.

Which Mentor Type?

What type of mentor style should you get; teacher, consultant or vested? All three styles offer great benefits and we continue to use all three. We've had the most personal success and have seen others enjoy the most success using the vested mentorship style, especially when learning something new. The reason is that when most people are starting out, extra money to build their Anti Suit life isn't as plentiful as they would like. Therefore, a Consultant style isn't always an option. The Teacher style requires unique relationships that most of us don't have at that point. It is also hard to maintain good exchanges with the mentor. How do you pay them back for their help? Charity only goes so far.

As you're learning something new, you "don't know what you don't know." Having a vested mentor who has some experience and success can help you tremendously by avoiding pit falls and helping you stay focused on the important activities. Since the vested mentor is vested on some level to how much success you have, he will be willing to mentor you up front because he'll get financially compensated for his time down the road, when you have success. With that thought in mind, don't expect every mentor to take you. As with everyone, they have limited time and do an ROLIFE (or similar) analysis for investing their time and resources.

Most mentors who are willing to become a vested mentor don't care how much success or experience you have in entrepreneurship or money in the bank. No, they care about your character, work ethic, level of commitment, and how coachable you are. That's what we look for as we mentor people. It's obvious why a mentor would not want to put time or effort into someone who is not willing to work hard, are lazy, or are not that serious about becoming an Anti Suit Entrepreneur. However, the idea that a vested mentor would look at how coachable a person is, may surprise you. If a person isn't willing to take advice, it's going to frustrate and waste the time of the vested mentor. If the vested mentor's advice is being ignored, he'll stop mentoring the person because he has better things to do with his time. He'll mentor someone else that gives him a better ROLIFE.

Finding a Mentor

As you search for a mentor, be very careful of various coaching, mentoring, and education companies out there. Some of these companies even have some very big names attached to them. We like to keep "our fingers on the pulse" of what it's like to be a new person entering into entrepreneurship. While we were revising this chapter, Chris went to a very popular coaching and education company's website, that also has a big name behind it, and filled out an online form. For legal and privacy reasons, we'll leave the company's name out of this book. More likely than not, you're familiar with the person behind the scenes at this company.

Within an hour of filling out the form, Chris received a phone call from one of the schedulers. He wasn't a mentor or coach, but he was calling to set up the appointment and do a qualification call. A qualification call is where they gauge how interested you are and how much money or credit you have. Almost immediately, Chris was asked these questions:

- "How much money do you have set aside to invest in this coaching program?"
- "Have you established credit with banks and credit card companies?"
- "How much credit do you have available?"

Chris answered the questions and was told, "Wonderful! You qualify to meet with one of our program directors who are the 'right hand men' of [Name removed; but it's a popular name.]"

That line of questioning sure makes one wonder if the company is more interested in helping you out or figuring out how much money they charge you for coaching. Without going into all the details, Chris spoke with one of the program directors and was told, "The level of coaching you need in order to have success will cost you $14,995. Are you ready to invest in yourself and your financial future?"

Chris laughed, said no, and hung up. That process and line of questioning is the typical sales process for these education and coaching companies. Here's our advice when it comes to those companies: **Stay the hell away from them! They are one small step above scam artists.** We cannot make the font bold enough or big enough in this book to emphasize that point! We're making a very strong and generalized statement because we've never met one person who has had success from these various education and coaching companies. Dozens of people have told us how much money they have wasted on those programs. Some of those same people, after following our advice on finding a vested mentor, have told us that they learned more from their vested mentor in a month than from a year in these $10,000+ coaching programs.

We wanted to share Chris's story and emphasize the point of staying away from those companies because we know how easy it is to get excited and then sucked into such a program. Now, let's talk about what to do in order to find a good vested mentor. There is no magic formula or "1-2-3 step" process to do.

Put your focus and attention on finding a vested mentor. Have you experienced a time when you were thinking about someone and then out of the blue they called or texted you? It's almost as though they read your mind. Or how about when you put your mind to something, things seem to fall into place? Putting mental energy and attention on finding a vested mentor has a funny way of connecting you with the right people.

Become proactive in seeking out ways to become an Anti Suit Entrepreneur. A gentleman, with whom we are now vested mentors, just finished a successful career as an IT executive and decided to become an entrepreneur because he wanted complete control over his schedule. In his search to find a business, he analyzed 57 different businesses with very thorough spreadsheet models. He was actively seeking out businesses, not vested mentors, in order to become an Anti Suit Entrepreneur. Once we got connected, we saw the potential in working with a hard working, serious and analytical person, and we approached him with the idea of vested mentorship. He quickly saw the value in the vested mentorship concept. We all have been working together for years and all have made money from the vested mentor relationship.

In college, after Chris put his mind on not working a traditional job, he was talking with a person in one of his classes who recommended a business book on entrepreneurship. Chris read the book and that set off a chain of events that eventually led him to meeting Jason and entering into a vested mentor relationship with him. As we wrote earlier, Jason mentored Chris and they both became more successful. Our vested mentorship relationship eventually turned into being business partners in a few different businesses. Chris can trace the chain of events all the way back to the book that someone recommended to him in college.

After Chris's chain of events from book to Anti Suit Entrepreneur success, we now always recommend to others that they talk with the person who recommended a book that struck a nerve with them. You never know where it might lead, as in Chris's case. If, by chance, someone recommended this book to you, we'd encourage you to talk with that person. Who knows how where that relationship may lead you.

ANTI⬤SUIT
CHARGE AHEAD
HOMEWORK

Get it. Read it. **Apply it.**

An Anti Suit Mentor can hold you accountable, make suggestions on your progress, and help you overcome the common obstacles that new entrepreneurs face. Setup your customized Anti Suit exit plan with an Anti Suit Mentor at www.AntiSuitEntrepreneur.com/chapter6

Chapter 7
Don't Drink the Positivity Kool-Aid

We want you to remember and ask yourself this question throughout your entrepreneurial journey, "Am I drinking the Positivity Kool-Aid?" The phrase "Positivity Kool-Aid" is one that we thought up and have used over the years to help us become successful Anti Suit Entrepreneurs. We came up with this question because it's very easy to get so caught up in the excitement of an idea, project, personal development seminar, or "living a 100% positive lifestyle," that it can actually stop or prevent you from developing the LIFE that you want. Over the years, we've actually seen people receive a negative impact in their life, finances, and entrepreneurial journey because they were *too* positive. Now, this idea that a person can be too positive may surprise you.

But it happens. That's part of the reason we came up with such a vivid phrase. Remembering to ask yourself, "Am I drinking the Positivity Kool-Aid?" will hopefully be easier to do!

Being positive and cutting out the negative areas in your life is preached by almost all personal development books, seminars, instructors, and many people in society. The underlying message from many of these sources and people is that always being positive is the most important aspect to success and happiness. They are wrong.

It's important that you understand our position on having a positive outlook on life and utilizing personal development and self help resources. We are believers in them because they are important for developing the LIFE you want. However, they are not the "end all, be all" for determining your success and happiness.

Warren Buffett, the world's most successful stock investor and one of the wealthiest people, didn't pick his good investments by having positive thoughts and hoping they would increase in value! No, he has a methodical strategy for picking what companies to invest in. He's a brilliant person who does his homework and works hard.

The rest of this chapter will discuss common traps that we've seen people fall into on their entrepreneurial journey. We're covering these traps so when you're potentially in a similar situation, it'll help give you insight into what to do and hopefully make you ask yourself, "Am I drinking the Positivity Kool-Aid?"

Trap #1: The Endless Personal Development Addiction

Each of us has a purpose and something to offer the world. Personal development can be very helpful in allowing us to reach our potential so we can make a difference. However, we have seen people get addicted to personal development. This addiction leads to an endless treadmill of personal development because the person always thinks he needs to attend the next seminar or read the next book before taking action and applying the knowledge learned. What good does it do you, if you are not taking action and applying what you have learned before jumping into the next course?

We have read books, taken courses, attended seminars, and have even been through personal development immersion type programs. Immersion programs are where you spend a weekend or longer in a group environment designed to facilitate and challenge you. The idea behind immersion type programs is to get you out of your day to day routine so you can quickly see what you need to work on to improve as an entrepreneur, as well as a person. These immersion events can be very good. We've received tremendous benefits from some of these immersion style programs.

Personal development seminars and immersion programs only make money if people are paying and attending the next course or program. So, they are constantly having to sell the next program in order to stay in business and make a profit. This system has the potential for creating a conflict of interest and an ugly side to personal development programs. We truly believe that most personal development programs want to help people; however, sometimes their need for staying in business or a salesperson making a commission can cause them to lose sight of their original intention of helping the person.

Jason attended an immersion program that really helped him. He had some personal breakthroughs and gained insight and knowledge that he could not only apply to his entrepreneurial journey, but also use for the rest of his life. Unfortunately, though, some staff members at the organization got more focused on selling the next program, rather than helping out the person. Jason was sitting in a room that had a few desks set up. Each desk had a salesperson talking with a program participant. The goal for each salesperson was to get his participant signed up and moving onto the next program.

The common message between the salesperson and the participant was, "I know you learned a lot from this program, but the next one is the big one! This is the game changer that will forever impact your life."

Jason told his salesperson, "I learned a lot from the program I just attended. I'm not going to sign up for the next program at this moment. I'm going to take what I learned and apply it to my life and business. I'll come back later to do the next program." That wasn't exactly what the salesperson wanted to hear, but Jason was firm and didn't deviate from his plan.

While in the room, Jason overheard the conversation at the next desk. He couldn't believe what he was hearing.

After the sales pitch for the next program, the salesperson asked for the sale and the participant replied, "I would love to do it, but I just don't have the money right now."

Salesperson: "Just put it on your credit card. I guarantee that after this program, you will be so powerful, you will make that money back right away."

Participant: "But, I already maxed out my credit card on the other programs!"

Salesperson: "So get another credit card and let's use it! Let's call American Express right now and get you a new card."

Jason was sitting there listening to this and thinking: "What? Guaranteeing you'll be able to pay it back from what you gain in the program? You maxed out your credit card on the previous programs? Get another credit card and charge it? What the hell is wrong with this salesperson and what is wrong with this person who is considering putting another course on a credit card?"

Then it hit Jason; the participant had drunk the "Positivity Kool-Aid" and was believing that the only way he could have success in life and business was by taking the next program from this organization. Part of Jason wanted to jump into the conversation and ask, "If you put earlier programs on your credit card, then based on what the salesperson said, shouldn't the knowledge and power that you gained from them allow you to pay off your credit card now without any issue?"

You may think that is an extreme example, but, unfortunately, it isn't.

There are numerous immersion and seminar personal development programs. Typically they have an initial $250 to $500 price tag which covers a two or three day weekend event. A few hundred dollars for a two or three day event is completely reasonable and usually a very good value for what you learn. While you're attending the event, you get very pumped up and excited at what you're learning. Typically, toward the end of the event, they sell you on the next event. The promise is that the next event will teach you even more and help you overcome more personal obstacles. Often times this next level costs $2,000 to $3,000. Then the cycle repeats itself. At the end of the second seminar, they will sell you on the next seminar, which not only teaches you more, but also costs two to five times more then the current program! Then there's a level after that and so on. We've heard of numerous programs that end up costing more than $10,000 per level, once you get past the first few.

Now, everyone is going to have a different opinion on whether or not the higher cost levels are worth it. We have come to two conclusions from our years of experience and common sense:

1) You should take time off between the levels or courses with personal development programs to actually implement the knowledge you learned.
2) If you haven't paid off the previous level or course yet, do **not** even think about putting the next course on your credit card, no matter what. Ideally, you should be paying cash for these programs anyhow.

It's very common for the organization to offer you a discount for the next course if you sign up before the current one ends. Even if they are offering an irresistible deal at the end of one course or level, you need to resist it. Saving $500 off of a $3,000 course may sound like a good savings, but you're still putting out $2,500! If the first course really gave you good knowledge and personal breakthroughs, then you should have no problem making up that $500 discount.

Personal development is a great resource that can help you reach your goal. We strongly encourage you to pursue your own personal development. However, remember to keep it all in perspective by asking yourself the question, "Am I drinking the Positivity Kool-Aid?" By asking this question, it'll hopefully allow you to step away from the moment, think about it, and put it into perspective with everything else in your busy life.

Stop for a minute before you continue reading and ask yourself, "Am I drinking the Positivity Kool-Aid in personal development?" Are you constantly attending the next seminar or reading book after book without taking time to apply the knowledge to your life? Are you on the treadmill of personal development or always "preparing to prepare"? An Anti Suit Entrepreneur understands that personal development is important, but without action, it's useless.

Trap #2: Being Positive Doesn't Pay the Bills, Action Does

In 2006 a self-help movie called *The Secret* was released. The movie was marketed incredibly well and created quite the buzz by promising to "reveal the single most powerful law in the universe..." that can change your life. *The Secret* is based on the law of attraction, which is a belief that "like attracts like." If a person focuses on positive thoughts, those thoughts will have a ripple effect throughout the universe and cause positive results for the person. The same holds true, if you have negative thoughts. The idea of the law of attraction, in some form or the other, has been around for a long time and written about in many different cultures.

Let's say you want your dream house on top of a cliff overlooking the ocean. Using the law of attraction, you would think about that house as if you already owned it and lived there. You would visualize yourself and your family enjoying the house. Your positive thinking, along with some visualization exercises, would cause a ripple effect throughout the universe to cause the house you want to manifest itself into your life. *The Secret* has numerous examples like this where people were able to think positive and attract different areas of wealth, health, relationships, and general happiness into their lives. All the examples are life changing and some are even life saving, when it came to some serious health issues people had.

Unfortunately, many people in the world have latched onto this concept and believe that all you need to do is think positive and visualize what you want, and the universe will deliver it to you. They drank the "Positivity Kool-Aid" when it came to positive thinking and the law of attraction, thinking that's all they needed to do for success! The bottom line is that you're not going to get what you want, unless you take action and work for it.

Before we're labeled as negative people, we want to be clear in our belief that positive thinking is an important aspect to achieving success and happiness. However, it's not the magic bullet. You still have to take action and work to get the desired results. Positive thinking doesn't pay the bills, action and work do. It doesn't matter how positive you are if you don't have money in the bank to pay your mortgage and credit card bill! Our belief is that you should be positive, but also be a realist.

A few years ago, Chris attended an entrepreneurship event. At this point, Chris was already well into his Anti Suit Entrepreneur journey and was generating a solid Diversified Cash Flow. The event had busses running between different venues and locations. Chris sat down on the bus next to a person and started a conversation. The person was very positive and upbeat about how "this year is going to be the year for my business!"

This intrigued Chris, "What's changed for you? What are your plans?"

The person replied, "For years now I haven't been motivated enough to build my business. I've had very little success in it, so I haven't been able to escape from my job. This past year I attended personal development seminars that helped me figure out what was holding me back. It changed my life. Now I'm ready to grow my business."

As he and Chris kept talking, Chris realized that he had actually attended the same personal development seminar. Chris went to a introductory seminar or level one seminar that cost a few hundred dollars for the weekend. Chris learned a few things from the seminar, but not enough for him to enroll into the next level that cost $2,000 or $3,000. There was nothing in there that was going to change his life or business. This person, however, had gone through all the levels of the personal development program. We don't know an exact figure, but had heard it was around $30,000 to attend all the levels. So, a very large chunk of money.

Chris was curious about what was taught at the higher levels and if it was really worth the price tag. Chris told him he attended the introductory seminar but didn't go beyond that and asked, "What did you learn from those seminars that you can apply to you business?"

The participant replied with energy, "That I need to get out there and make it happen!"

Chris asked, "What specifically are you going to do to make it happen and grow your business?"

What Chris heard back surprised him, "I don't know... but I'm going to make it happen. I know I can. This will be the year!"

Chris liked the guy and wanted to pass along a few tips to hopefully help him grow his business. Chris started sharing some marketing strategies he had run in the past. As they got into detail, the person said, "That sounds great and all, but I can't afford that. My credit cards are maxed out from the personal development seminar."

Once they reached their destination and parted ways, Chris couldn't help but wonder what that $30,000 would have done for the person's business, if it was actually spent on the business rather than on personal development seminars. Although people make their own bed with their choices, Chris couldn't help but feel sorry for this person. He was positive, he was happy, and he seemed like a good guy. But, how long is that positivity going to last without any measurable results? Being positive with a "make it happen" attitude, maxed out credit cards, and no money to advertise your business is not a business plan! It's a recipe for disaster and for not becoming an Anti Suit Entrepreneur.

Chris really hoped that things somehow did work out for the aspiring entrepreneur, but odds were stacked against him. When you look at the fact that this person has been working on his business for years, hasn't realized any success, and has attended multiple programs spending in excess of $30,000 with this one company (and who knows what else this person has done over the years), and he still looks at this next year with optimism, it makes us wonder what in the world he was thinking. If this person hasn't been doing any action to this point, it leads us to believe that he will continue to work on being positive, which isn't going to help him achieve his entrepreneurial goals.

We're all about being positive, but we make sure that we stay in reality and take action so we can pay the bills!

One of Jason's friends got infatuated with the *The Secret* and the law of attraction. She was an extremely talented and smart girl, but had a very lazy work ethic. Once she watched *The Secret*, she became a very empowered individual, despite her own lack of success. She started thinking positive and visualizing her success, but didn't take any action. Then she started telling Jason that he "focused on the negative too much and needed to be more positive."

At this point in Jason's life, he was already very successful with a strong Diversified Cash Flow. He found it ironic that someone who has never accomplished anything is suddenly giving advice to someone who has accomplished a lot. Jason had no issue with her lack of success yet or that she was thinking positive. He had an issue with her lecturing him about it. He also found it ironic that a person implementing *The Secret's* teaching focused on the negativity in someone else's life, which goes completely against the law of attraction!

Needless to say, that friendship didn't last much longer. Jason was willing to mentor her and help her out, but couldn't do so since she drank the "Positivity Kool-Aid."

These two stories really signify how positivity without action can go wrong and derail a person's entrepreneurial journey. In the first story the person set himself up for failure. In the second, Jason's friend drove away a friend and potential mentor. Remember to think positive, but make sure you take action so you can pay your bills at the end of the month.

Trap #3: Being Realistic Doesn't Necessarily Make You "Negative"

Have you ever been around a group who started to discuss an idea that was so exciting that the group got stuck in groupthink (meaning that no one is slowing down to evaluate the situation)? Sometimes the best ideas come out of nowhere, and a group understandably gets excited, caught up in the moment, and charges ahead on the idea. This is good, because we have harped so much on taking action, but it also shows the other side of the coin on positivity without action. Some people are so positive, they take action without any analysis.

We will be the first to say that we often follow the "ready, fire, aim" (as opposed to the normal "ready, aim, fire") philosophy in some of our entrepreneurial endeavors, but we always stop to make sure we are on the right track and not drinking the "Positivity Kool-Aid" to our own detriment. We may not try to figure everything out before taking action, but we try to evaluate on the surface the potential problems that may arise in a new, exciting project.

All the excitement and energy moving forward can prevent the group from seeing potential issues with the project or plan. Healthy functioning groups should welcome questions and debate among its members to help ensure success. But in this era of positive thinking and self-help books, a lot of people have taken it so far that it's almost socially unacceptable to present opinions, concerns, or ask questions in those situations. This line of thinking can cause the group to label the person as a negative or not on board with the group's goal. This chance of being called negative causes a lot of people to not speak up.

We have spoken up at times in groups about potential issues and have been labeled negative. From our perspective, we weren't being negative, but rather realistic regarding potential issues and obstacles. We call that being smart and savvy. It's important to be able to stop in the moment and analyze the situation you're in, regardless of what people will label you. If you move forward with the group and things go south, it can impact your life and your business. It's important to be able to stop and ask yourself, "Am I drinking the Positivity Kool-Aid from this group?"

There was a project that was brought to us by a successful entrepreneur. He had gotten in touch with the creator of a green cleaning and disinfectant product that was "More effective than bleach, yet as safe as water." That claim certainly caught our attention! For the sake of this story, we'll label the entrepreneur pitching the idea to the group as the project leader. We'll label another entrepreneur in the group as the project follower because he followed the project leader blindly, much like a labrador dog following his master around.

There were a few other people involved, but we'll leave them out for example's sake.

We were intrigued and excited with the idea that the project leader presented. Before we would invest much time and money and associate our names on it, we had to do our due diligence. Even though we respected the project leader, we were not wired to blindly follow him into a new business venture. Our need for due diligence wasn't about trust. It was about coming to our own conclusions. Maybe the project leader believed in his heart that it was a great product, but maybe this belief was based on poor evaluation. The point is, as business people, we should always do our own evaluation.

The first thing we wanted to do was try and use the product for ourselves. If we didn't like the product, there was no way we would get involved with it, no matter how good it was. The project leader said he would try to get some, but it would be a challenge.

A few weeks went by and the project leader still couldn't get us any product to try, yet he always seemed to have an endless supply of the product in plastic bottles he bought from the store. One day when Chris was at the project leader's house, he said, "I'm very excited and interested in this, but I need to try the product. You seem to have a lot on hand. Why can't I get any?"

The project leader hesitated for a moment and then said, "Okay, give me your credit card." The project leader then opened up his laptop, went to a website, and ordered five gallons for Chris.

Chris was happy he would get some so both of us could try it out. However, Chris got quite a surprise when the box arrived on his door step. There was already a company and distributor behind the product! The one gallon bottles were labeled and the receipt gave a website address so more product could be ordered.

Needless to say, it surprised both us to find a finished product with a company behind it! At the next group meeting, Chris asked the project leader about this, "I'm confused and lost. How is this product already out in the market and available for purchase?"

The project leader replied, "That brand with that label of the product is already out there. You see, however, we're going to create a different brand and label for it and distribute it that way." He then proceeded to change the subject. Chris started to ask another question about not having exclusive distribution rights, but felt a tap on his shoulder and a look of "quiet down" from the project follower. Chris sat through the rest of the meeting silently and started analyzing the product from the new perspective of not having exclusive distribution rights to it. From what we could tell, it just wasn't adding up to a good business deal. But everyone in the group was on board and excited!

Over the next couple of meetings, the same scenario kept playing out where Chris would ask a question, not get a satisfactory answer, and then get shunned by the group for asking more questions. Just to be clear, Jason wasn't at any of these meetings, as Chris represented the both of us. After this scenario happened a few times, we decided that we needed to get answers to all of our questions or we were going to pull away.

At the next meeting Chris was vocal about his questions to the project leader, "So, how is this going to work exactly when there is an already established brand out there that we would essentially be competing against?"

The project leader, visibly irritated, replied, "Like I told you before, we'll develop a different brand name for it. Rather than selling it at high concentrations in one gallon jugs, we'll dilute the product down and put it in smaller, more convenient bottles. We'll create different bottles for different tasks from cleaning the kitchen to getting rid of smells. We'll eventually incorporate other products into the mix as well." It was obvious that he wanted Chris to shut up and fall in line.

This plan made no sense to Chris on all sorts of levels and he started firing off questions, "Won't people just figure out that it's the same product as the concentrated stuff and buy that? I can't honestly recommend and sell a diluted product that costs more when I know there is a better deal available! Can you? If the product developer is allowing us to sell the product under a different brand, how many other people are going to do this in the future?"

The project leader couldn't give any satisfactory answers to our questions. We pulled away from the group and took ourselves out of the project. However, no one else did, even after all of the questions and points were raised. The project leader was a brilliant salesperson and great at getting people to buy into his ideas. Unfortunately, the other people in the group were "drinking the Positivity Kool-Aid." Fortunately, we had enough experience in entrepreneurship to do our due diligence and analyze the situation. We're very glad we did because the project ended up going nowhere.

Months after we stepped away from the project, we heard that the project leader ended up presenting the product to an incredibly smart scientist who happened to have different businesses and charities in the areas of helping people live healthier lives. He's a very influential figure. He's also a shrewd businessman. He shot down the project leader's idea for a variety of reasons.

Hearing that result validated the problems we saw. It also made us very appreciative that we were able to stop and ask ourselves, "Are we drinking the Positivity Kool-Aid?" Doing that analysis helped us avoid investing months, and who knows how much money, into that project that went nowhere.

This story represents a typical situation where being realistic can be viewed as negative. The demeanor of the other two parties clearly indicated that cautious questioning wasn't allowed. It was sit, listen, and agree with what we are doing.

So when you think of the result, was it negative for Chris to ask these questions or was Chris being realistic? What made Chris feel as though it was wrong to ask the question? He was "hushed" by one of the parties. Before this project ever hit, the follower had previous dealings with Jason, and he would often come up with an idea and Jason would ask questions in a very similar fashion to Chris's questions. The follower would often say, "You're just being negative."

The point we are making with this story is: Being a realist doesn't make you negative. In fact, it makes you a smart and savvy entrepreneur. Work with groups that are able to look at exciting ideas with a positive, but critical eye. If people in a group are not willing to answer your questions, that should raise a red flag for you.

Are You Drinking The Positivity Kool-Aid?

We hope that by sharing these stories you can glean some wisdom from them and apply it to your life and future situations. Utilizing personal development and thinking positive are important steps in becoming an Anti Suit Entrepreneur. That's why, at the beginning of the chapter, we asked you to remember and ask yourself throughout your entrepreneurial journey, "Am I drinking the Positivity Kool-Aid?"

We've been in situations where the thought of "drinking Positivity Kool-Aid" pops in our minds. The image always brings a chuckle to us and helps us break away from the moment, so we can reflect and do some analysis. Hopefully, it'll help you avoid getting sucked into the endless personal development treadmill or being afraid to speak up and ask questions in groups.

ANTI⬤SUIT
CHARGE AHEAD
HOMEWORK

Get it. Read it. **Apply it.**

Don't get caught by the Personal Development Traps; download your Trap Reminder Sheet that you can hang in your office, so you never get "off-track" while you are on your Anti Suit Entrepreneur journey. Download our Personal Development Traps Reminder List at www.AntiSuitEntrepreneur.com/chapter7

Chapter 8

Your Health is Critical to Living Life on Your Terms

The Dalai Lama was asked what surprised him most about humanity. He replied, "Man. Because he sacrifices his health in order to make money. Then he sacrifices money to recuperate his health. And then he is so anxious about the future that he does not enjoy the present; the result being that he does not live in the present or the future; he lives as if he is never going to die, and then dies having never really lived."

This chapter on health may seem out of place to you because, traditionally, one doesn't associate discussing health with entrepreneurship. However, the quote from the

Dalai Lama sums up perfectly what happens to many entrepreneurs: their health gets sacrificed in their entrepreneurial journey. We don't want that to happen to you. To us, not incorporating the importance of staying healthy, while discussing entrepreneurship, is crazy! In fact, they go hand in hand because, if you don't have good health, you cannot truly live life on your terms. By staying healthy, you'll also get a better ROLIFE because you'll be happier, more productive, and generate more cash flow into your bank account.

What's the point of working hard to become an Anti Suit Entrepreneur and living life on your terms, if you won't have your health to enjoy it? The answer is obvious: it's not worth it. We've never met a person who disagreed with this point. Yet, many people end up taking their health for granted, until they no longer have good health, and it's too late. Then all the money in the world doesn't matter. We call this the catastrophic health nightmare. A catastrophic health nightmare is when a person has a life changing health issue, such as a stroke or cancer, or dies at an early age.

A catastrophic health nightmare will put a quick end to living life on your terms. Now, no one wants to experience a catastrophic health nightmare, but unfortunately it happens. With Jason's law background, he heard story after story of lawyers busting their butts, sacrificing time with their families, and putting off taking care of their health in order to build successful law careers, only to have a catastrophic health nightmare in their 40's or 50's. He noticed that no matter how successful they were or how much money they had, they and their families were never the same again. Those experiences drove home the point to him that money is useless without health.

A major goal of an Anti Suit Entrepreneur is to have money *and* health so he can live life on his terms.

The Rigors of the Entrepreneurial Transition

Maintaining your health while becoming an entrepreneur is often easier said than done. In order to pay the bills, many aspiring entrepreneurs still work another job, which is a financially smart move. However, this extra work can put a squeeze on an already too busy schedule, that is full of work, family, and personal commitments. To fit more into your schedule, such as entrepreneurial commitments, you either have to become more efficient and/or drop other commitments from your schedule. Often, time devoted to working out and staying healthy is one of the first commitments to get bumped off the schedule. Skipping one day turns into a couple of days, then a week, then a couple of weeks and, before you know it, months or even years have gone by without working out or focusing on staying healthy! We don't need to go into detail about how that life style usually leads to pounds getting added on and health taking a hit.

Here's the bottom line, no matter how busy your schedule is, you have to figure out a way to stay healthy while you're on your entrepreneurial journey for two main reasons:

- Staying healthy will help minimize the chance of a catastrophic health nightmare.
- The healthier you are, the greater the increase in your ROLIFE (Return on LIFE).

Catastrophic health nightmares are not completely avoidable. However, there have been enough studies over the years that have proved how staying healthy by eating well, exercising, and minimizing stress can help people live longer and avoid major catastrophic health nightmares. We're not going to spend time referencing those studies, since it's generally accepted as common knowledge today. All we'll do is remind you that money is useless without health. So, maintain your health the best you can to help avoid catastrophic health nightmares.

The second point of having a greater increase in your ROLIFE may surprise you, as it has many other people over the years.

How People Perceive You Will Affect You

When Jason was in law, he worked with a lawyer from Europe who was in his 40's and had lived in the U.S. for about 10 years. This European lawyer wasn't a health fanatic or gym rat, but he had a very interesting and different point of view on health than do many Americans. He didn't understand how Americans could be so unhealthy and out of shape as a society. One day he said to Jason, "If someone cannot take care of themselves, how are they going to take care of their responsibilities to me?" In other words, he avoided doing business with people who looked unhealthy. This comment took Jason by surprise, but as he thought about it, he could understand the European lawyer's point of view.

Some people will resist this concept, but it's true; healthier looking people are more impressive than unhealthy looking people. Does this mean that a healthy looking person is better than an unhealthy looking person? No. Does it mean that unhealthy looking people are automatically inferior to healthy looking people? No, of course not. But, perception is reality.

This topic reminds us of the saying, "Don't judge a book by its cover." One cannot know how great or poor a book is until it's read. How the cover looks certainly influences a person's inclination to read or not read the book. It could be the greatest book in the world, but if the cover is horrible and turns people off from actually reading it, the book won't get the recognition it deserves. You can draw the parallels from this metaphor to healthy looking and unhealthy looking people being "judged by their cover."

We're not saying that this is politically correct or right or wrong. We're being transparent with you about how some people perceive healthy looking and unhealthy looking people. Understand that you may be judged by "your cover" of how healthy or unhealthy you look. Others' perceptions of you have the potential to increase or decrease your ROLIFE.

You Will Be Happier

There is a strong connection between exercising, eating well, and staying healthy and a person's mood. We don't need to cite studies to prove this. As with us, you've probably experienced feelings of anxiety or anger that have ruined your day or put you into a bad mood. Once you exercise, the feelings seem to magically melt away, at least partially, and you're put into a happier mood!

Obviously, this improvement is good for your own well being and your relationships. Think about how your mood can impact your work or people with whom you're talking. We've all snapped at or treated someone poorly, not because they deserved it, but because we were in a bad mood. We've also all been around those people who are upbeat and happy who have rubbed off on us and elevated our own moods!

If you're interacting or dealing with people in your entrepreneurial venture, how much is your bad mood costing you? How much is your good mood making you? There's really no way to assign a dollar value to this, but we're sure that you can agree with the general rule of thumb. What happens if you're in a bad mood and you turn off a potential vested mentor? How much could that potential relationship be worth?

You Will Have More Aha Moments

The Merriam Webster Dictionary defines an aha moment as "a moment of sudden realization, inspiration, insight, recognition, or comprehension." In our experience, the more you exercise, the more aha moments you'll have. Our years of being Anti Suit Entrepreneurs have proven that to us. There have been countless times where we've been working on a project or a piece of marketing and have hit a dead end. No matter how much time we put into it, we just couldn't get it figured out. Once we stepped away and worked out, we had the aha moment!

We're not sure of how the mind and body work together in those situations to produce those results, but we don't really care how. We're just glad that it does. One of our rules now is step away from a project on which we are stuck and go workout, no matter what time of the day or how close we are to the deadline. We don't always get an aha moment while exercising, but regardless, working out does help get the project done more quickly and efficiently. Even if no aha moment occurs, exercising helps to clear the mind and get us back to work feeling refreshed.

Making yourself stop and go work out can be extremely hard because you get sucked into the project and don't want to walk away until you get that problem figured out. Routinely, we call each other out on this. It's easy for one of us to see that the other is stuck and tell him that he needs to exercise. A mentor or a community can help you out tremendously in these challenging situations.

We highly recommend that you make working out a rule when you're stuck. Without a doubt, working out has helped us have more aha moments, which has helped us achieve a better ROLIFE.

You Will Get More Done

The Department of Labor conducted a review in 2012 on workplace wellness programs. In this review, four studies evaluated the impact of wellness programs on productivity in the workplace. The studies wanted to calculate how much employees' illnesses, and the resulting loss of productivity and sick days, were costing the employers. All four studies found significant savings from the wellness programs. The wellness programs provided an ROI (Return on Investment) of $15.60 for every wellness dollar spent. It's extremely impressive to see that every dollar spent on a wellness program saved the company $15.60!

If corporations are investing money into their employees' health in order to increase productivity and save money, shouldn't you be doing the same as an entrepreneur? Of course you should! Now, you probably won't be able to calculate a specific dollar amount that you'll be saving. However, we can tell you from our 10 plus years as Anti Suit Entrepreneurs, that staying healthy has saved us money, increased productivity, and helped us create a bigger Diversified Cash Flow.

We hardly ever get sick and when we do, we don't get knocked too much out of commission. We take fewer sick days and don't get slowed down as many people do. This healthfulness is particularly important when you're starting out as an entrepreneur because until you have a significant recurring income established, your time is money. If you can't put time into your entrepreneurial venture, then you're not making active income.

We also have more energy, which allows us to get more done and be more productive. Many people are amazed at how much we accomplish. One of the reasons we get so much done is because we are very healthy and invest a lot in our own version of wellness programs, the Anti Gimmick Health Plan. This plan and a dedication to staying healthier can increase your ROLIFE!

The Anti Gimmick Health Plan

As you're aware, this is not a medical or health book. We are not medical or health professionals. So, make sure you consult with a medical professional before incorporating any of our advice into your life. Before we started our entrepreneurial journeys, both of us had a strong interest in fitness and nutrition. We've stayed in shape our entire lives by playing sports, being "gym rats," and leading very active lifestyles. Through our years of working on the marketing side of the nutrition industry, we've worked with various medical doctors, Olympic athletes, and medical and health professionals. These relationships have given us a very unique insight and perspective into health.

We enjoy learning about new health topics and then running informal experiments on ourselves to see what, if any, differences we feel in our day to day energy, well being, health, and productivity. We enjoy and have fun learning and experimenting on ourselves. There's always more to learn and more to try.

Based on our informal experiments and on what we have learned from our various contacts, we've put together the Anti Gimmick Health Plan. This is a plan or set of guidelines to help us stay healthy while we're busy with our entrepreneurial ventures. We've incorporated the 80/20 rule into the plan as well. This plan focusses on the areas that give the best return on staying healthy. We call it the Anti Gimmick Health Plan because we got so tired of all the hype, magic pills, diet of the month, and fad products of the week.

Our plan has helped us, and many of friends with whom we've shared it, keep on track with staying healthy. Hopefully you can get a nugget or two of information to help you stay healthy as you become an Anti Suit Entrepreneur.

The Anti Gimmick Health Plan is made up of four areas:

- Exercise
- Accountability
- Eating Right
- Nutritional Supplementation

Exercise

The importance of exercise is well known. The key to exercising is finding something that you can fit into your schedule and that you enjoy. Don't get caught up in what's the best way to exercise or the latest craze. Focus on something that you enjoy and can consistently do three to five times a week.

We incorporate resistance, cardiovascular, and flexibility training into our exercise routines. All three are extremely important, however flexibility may surprise you. Flexibility is critical in injury prevention and helping you to stay healthy, especially if you spend a lot of time at a desk or behind a computer. Many of the medical and health professionals with whom we have worked talk about how sitting behind a desk for eight or more hours a day is not what human bodies were designed for! Maintaining flexibility will help people who sit behind desks keep their backs and bodies limber and healthy.

A common misconception among women is that if they do resistance training, they will bulk up like body builders, so they avoid it. Listen ladies, you're not going to turn into a body builder by doing some resistance training! Both men and women who develop very muscular physiques spend years training and following a strict diet to get a body like that. Women doing normal resistance training have nothing to worry about.

If your schedule is too full and you can't make it to the gym, don't let that be an excuse for not exercising. There are numerous ways you can fit some exercise into your schedule, such as taking the stairs instead of the elevator, doing ten pushups or squats when time allows, or walking the dog while returning phone calls. Doing a little bit is much better than doing nothing! When your schedule gets slammed, try to figure out ways to squeeze in exercise.

Accountability

It's easy to get sidetracked from goals, especially health goals, since they often get pushed down to the bottom of the to-do list. Accountability is critical in helping people change their habits and in maintaining their health. Just as you need a mentor for your Anti Suit Entrepreneurship journey, you need some form of accountability or mentorship when it comes to health.

There are different ways one can be held accountable when it comes to staying healthy. There's no best method for staying accountable. The best method is whatever works for you and helps you stay on track. Some people hire personal trainers at the gym to create workout plans and then walk them through the workout to make sure they do it. Other people have a gym buddy with whom to exercise. Having a gym buddy can be especially useful if you have early morning gym workouts because no one likes letting s friend down by not showing up at 6 A.M.! Keeping a journal or workout log is all the accountability that some people need. Other people get their accountability by participating in online forums or websites. Even though everyone might be spread out across the country, the online community and relationships are strong enough to hold them accountable. Others achieve accountability by such thoughts as appearing in a bathing suit in the coming months. That prospect can be a real motivator!

Can we recommend which you should do? No, we cannot. That's something you need to figure out. More likely than not, you know what you need to do in order to be held accountable to health and fitness goals. All we can recommend is that you get into the habit of being held accountable because study after study has shown that people who are held accountable get more results than those who are not.

Eating Right

We're not into the fad diet of the month that the media constantly churns out. We're into eating habits that are easy to follow and that fuel the brain and the body. We are both very in tune with our bodies and notice a difference in how we feel and in our productivity when we make changes. We won't go into full details or meal plans because that is outside the scope of this book. We will cover a few general principles that have helped us stay trim, full of energy, and productive.

The foundation of our eating habits is the glycemic index. This index is a rating system that lets you know how fast carbohydrates break down and raise the body's blood sugar levels. It rates foods on a scale from zero to 100. The higher the number, the faster the food raises the blood sugar levels. Think about when you've eaten a big bowl of ice cream or a bunch of candy and you have the "sugar rush" and then the "sugar crash." Ice cream and candy are high-glycemic foods that raise the blood sugar quickly. Generally, when you eat those they get you on a hunger roller coaster for the rest of the day where you crave more high glycemic foods. Spiking blood sugar levels wreak havoc on your metabolism, energy levels, and productivity throughout the day. The 2 P.M. "I need a nap" crash, that many people experience, does not enhance productivity!

Focusing on a low-glycemic index, or slow carb eating habits, is the ticket to not getting those uncontrollable hunger cravings and energy crashes throughout the day. Following low-glycemic index eating habits allows us to have consistent energy and mental focus throughout the day, which, in turn, allows us to be more productive and have plenty of energy for work and exercise.

There is no specific brand or store from which you must buy from in order to enjoy the benefits of low-glycemic index eating. Also, it is easy and free to find out the glycemic index rating of each food. In fact, you can find all the information you need about eating low-glycemic foods on the Internet for free.

We highly encourage you to spend some time researching the glycemic index and eating low-glycemic foods. We're confident that you'll get a better ROLIFE, as we have, if you incorporate the glycemic index into your eating habits.

Nutritional Supplementation

There is no magic pill, despite the promises from the constant barrage of new products and their outrageous health claims. Nutritional supplements are not replacements for eating well and exercise. Rather, nutritional supplements are designed and intended to help people *supplement* their diet. We are big believers in incorporating high quality, science driven nutritional supplements into the Anti Gimmick Health Plan. We're also strong believers in avoiding the magic pill or hype driven supplements with the big health claims.

Taking a multivitamin each day is at the top of our Anti Gimmick Health Plan. There are five reasons for this important habit.

Reason #1 - No matter how busy we are with life or a hectic travel schedule, we can always take a multivitamin. We cannot always eat right or fit exercise into our daily schedules, but we can always fit taking a multivitamin supplement into our schedules.

Reason #2 - There are numerous studies showing that people do not get enough vitamins and minerals. In 2001 the USDA surveyed 16,000 Americans and found that not even one person obtained 100% of essential nutrients, such as magnesium, vitamin E, and zinc.

Reason #3 - Farming and food production is now big business and big profits. Too often, farming is now about quantity rather than quality because the more production, the bigger the profits. There are numerous documentaries that shine a spotlight on these agricultural changes.

Reason #4 - There are more pollution and chemicals in our environment than ever before. Even if you're able to eat a completely organic diet, it's impossible to avoid all the pollution. Antioxidants, which come from healthy foods and nutritional supplements, help combat the effects of pollution on the human body.

Reason #5 - After starting to take a high quality multivitamin, we felt a difference in our day to day health. The difference we experienced was similar to feeling healthier and having more energy when we got into a good exercise routine and healthy eating habits. The bottom line is that if we notice a difference between when we do and do not take supplements, they are having a positive impact on our bodies and health.

These five reasons we went over are brief and to the point. It's our hope that they will encourage you to either incorporate a multivitamin into your plan or to, at least, do your own research. Below are a couple of tips to help you find a high quality multivitamin or any nutritional supplement.

Tip #1 - Is the company a credible and science based company? Go to their website to get a feel for the company. Does the website reference any science or is it all just marketing hype? Does it have a research and development department? Can you get your questions answered by someone at the company?

Tip #2 - Is there third party testing and verification of the products? Various independent organizations will test products to see if what is on the label is actually in the product. Informed-choice.org, a quality assurance program for sports nutrition, conducted a study in 2007 that found that about 25% of supplements could be contaminated with banned substances, such as steroids and stimulants, that could cause an athlete to test positive on a drug test! Consumerlabs.com and NSF.org are reputable organizations.

Tip #3 - Who is actually manufacturing the product and at what quality level? Many supplement companies do not make their own supplements, rather they outsource production to another company. Outsourcing is a great way to cut expenses, but it also opens the door for quality control issues as well. We also recommend getting products from a FDA registered facility because that means the manufacturing facility meets the same stringent quality control requirements of pharmaceutical and over the counter drugs.

Tip #4 - Do you feel or notice a difference? Keep in mind that you probably won't feel a difference immediately when taking a nutritional supplement. Many of the doctors we've worked with recommended taking the products for six months in order to get the full benefits. After years of taking supplements, if we skip even a few days, we feel it!

Creating Your Plan

A common objection we hear is that people are too busy to stay healthy. You must figure it out and find time to stay healthy. Jason figured out a way when he started down his Anti Suit Entrepreneur journey. At the time he was working full time and going to law school at night. He was extremely busy and stressed, but he made time. Many times he ended up going to the gym at 11 P.M.! Even though he was going late and sacrificing sleep, the workouts more than made up for it in terms of his mood, energy levels, and productivity.

Everyone is at a different stage when it comes to their health. Don't compare yourself to others or try to make a bunch of changes at once. Pick one or two areas and take baby steps toward improving those areas. Generally, when people try to make too many changes at once, they get overwhelmed and just set themselves up for failure.

Hopefully, the information we shared with you in this chapter will help you take a step or two in the right direction in regards to your health. We just cannot stress enough to you about how much staying healthy has helped us get a better ROLIFE and living life on our terms. Don't let bad health take away the life you want and the life you will get with the Anti Suit Entrepreneur philosophy. Remember, money means nothing without health.

ANTI⏀SUIT
CHARGE AHEAD
HOMEWORK

Get it. Read it. **Apply it.**

Set up your Customized Anti Gimmick Health Plan at www.AntiSuitEntrepreneur.com/chapter8

Chapter 9

Why Most Goal Setting is Unproductive

When Chris started down the path of becoming an Anti Suit Entrepreneur, he set the goal of "Making $100,000 a year by graduation to avoid getting a job." He had about two and a half years to go from knowing nothing about business and having very little income to earning a $100,000 a year. Tough? Yes. Realistic? Yes, according to all the goal setting books and gurus that he studied.

Chris laid out his plan to achieve his goal: He'd make $20,000 his first year, $50,000 his next and then $100,000 by the end of the third year. He did daily affirmations and visualization exercises, too, so he would stay focused on his goal. He did all the typical things that people are supposed to do in order to achieve their goals.

Guess what? He failed. You can probably relate with what happened to him and what he went through. Think back to goals that you've set in the past.

Things usually start off great because you get pumped up and focused on achieving your goals. You do all the right things by writing your goals out on index cards that you look at daily, visualizing your results, and telling everyone what your goals are. But then, something doesn't go according to plan. You miss one of the sub-goals to your bigger goal, the timeline isn't happening as you had planned, or life throws you an unexpected curve ball. You shake it off, get refocused, and start anew at your goal. Then it happens again; you get side tracked from your goal plan.

This pattern can only happen so many times until you start doubting yourself or second guessing your goals. The "downward spiral" starts occurring when one thing leads to another and another, until you eventually just scrap your goal and feel like a failure. If you've ever set goals before, then you've experienced that feeling and the following disaster of not achieving them.

Once you're on the "downward spiral," it's very hard to get off. It's strong and powerful in how it can derail you from achieving your goals. The "downward spiral" doesn't just affect that one goal, it affects everything you do after that. The next time you set a goal, you have in the back of your mind that you failed before and will probably fail again. It can turn real nasty, real fast. It can turn into a long term "downward spiral," lasting for years or even decades. Eventually, some people even give up on their goals for good and live a life of mediocrity, which is one of the saddest things that can happen to a person's life.

We're taught that if we don't achieve our goal, it's our fault, and we're to blame. However, when the majority of people who set goals don't achieve them, who or what is really at fault? The real culprit is the way you're taught to set goals. To put it clearly, the traditional method for setting goals has some serious flaws that actually set people up for failure before they even begin!

Once Chris composed himself after his "downward spiral" with goal setting, he started analyzing what went right, what went wrong, and what successful people were doing.

Sh*t Happens

Ever notice how life doesn't go according to plan? Like, never! This is one of the problems with traditional goal setting. It sets out a structured plan that looks great on paper, but doesn't work in the real world. No matter how focused you are on your goals, life is going to throw you a curve ball (or a dozen) that throws you off balance. We have never met a person who has not encountered some of life's curve balls. We're not just talking about the big life curve balls, such as family emergencies, loss of job, or buying a new house. It's the little curve balls that happen throughout the week that derail most people. The little curve balls are the little things that happen that mess up your schedule and plans. For example, getting stuck in traffic that throws off the rest of your day, coming down with a cold that slows you down for a couple of days, having out of town guests stay with you, or having to pick up a sick child from school early. How many curve balls have you had thrown at you just in this past week? Probably a few!

With traditional goal setting, every curve ball throws you off your plan just a little. Then you get behind on your plan, get frustrated, and start feeling like a failure because you can never stick to your goal setting plan! Then you start down the "downward spiral..."

Rather than trying to make your life, which is full of curve balls and sh*t happens moments, fit a goal setting plan, doesn't it make more sense to have a goal setting plan that fits the chaos of life? We think so... That's exactly why we created the Zig Zag Goal Setting methodology.

Zig Zag Goal Setting

The Zig Zag Goal Setting methodology is a system for setting your goals so they actually fit into your life in a way that you can achieve them and avoid the "downward spiral." When we first started teaching this concept years ago, we were floored by the response we received from people. They absolutely loved the concept! However, most importantly, people achieved more of their goals with less stress.

The Zig Zag Goal Setting methodology is built around the premise that nothing goes according to plan and life will constantly throw you curve balls. Once people embrace and utilize this methodology, stress is almost immediately reduced because there is no longer that friction from trying to make your life fit into a perfectly laid out plan. We have literally heard people breathe a sigh of relief and look as though a weight has been lifted from their shoulders! All of this was achieved from just learning the effective way to set goals.

Here's the interesting thing from all the successful people with whom we have talked with and observed; they are actually doing the Zig Zag Method, whether they realize it or not. Most successful people talk about setting goals using the traditional method, but end up doing the Zig Zag Method to actually achieve them.

Traditional goal setting has you set a goal and then create a plan for how you'll get there. If you were to draw it out, it would be a straight line on paper because it assumes your life will go as planned without any curve balls (which we know doesn't happen).

TRADITIONAL GOAL SETTING

FINISH

START

The best way to understand the Zig Zag Goal Setting methodology is to look at a maze that a young child would complete in school. There's a starting point and an ending point. If you can remember doing a maze when you were a child, you know it's not a straight line between the two. You had to make left turns and right turns to get to the end of the maze. There were probably some times that you even hit a dead end in the maze and had to trace your way back out and keep trying. Take a second and visualize what that maze would look like (or if you have a child, go look at one of his or hers!).

The chaos of completing the maze with left turns, right turns, and dead ends is the perfect example of how successful people achieve goals. All the changes in direction represent a curve ball from life or learning something new and adjusting how you'll achieve your goal. Part of the issue with setting goals is that "you don't know, what you don't know."

"ZIG ZAG"
METHOD
FINISH

START

It's impossible to plan out every step using the traditional goal setting method because you can't plan for things that you don't know even exist yet! As you're moving forward toward your goal, you'll start realizing what you don't know and make adjustments. There's nothing wrong with not knowing everything; just understand that it's a fact of life and it's a part of the process. Despite all the twists and turns, you will achieve your goal, just as you eventually get to the end of the maze. It may not happen the way you anticipated, but you do get there.

The twists and turns of completing the maze represent the zigging and zagging that one must do in order to achieve his goals in life. Think back to the goals you did achieve. Did everything go according to plan? No. If you reflect, you'll probably start noticing the left and right turns and dead ends that you ran into! You were probably zig zagging without realizing it!

Two Steps Forward, One Step Back

Understand that as you work toward your goal, you'll often take "two steps forward, one step back." Since you'll be working toward goals in areas that are new to you, you'll have quite a few "you don't know what you don't know moments," which is fine! This process falls in line with the concepts of Failing Forward and "action trumps perfection" from the Anti Suit Mindset chapter. Another important reason for developing your mindset is that it'll help you with achieving your goals.

Imagine you're driving in an unfamiliar city and you get lost. You know what road you're on, but don't know where exactly you are on the road or in what direction you're going. You have to keep driving until you hit a cross street, so you can figure out your direction and location. You may realize that you're driving in the wrong direction and that you need to make a u-turn to get headed in the right direction. You can only get back on the correct road by driving and moving forward. You'll never know what direction you're going, if you're standing still on the side of the road.

The same concept exists for when you're working toward your goals. You have to keep moving forward so you know what adjustments you need to make. You can't figure out your direction if you're standing still! Sometimes that'll cause you to take "two steps forward and one step back." So *when* (not *if*) you hit a setback, don't let that get you flustered or frustrated. Actually, have the exact opposite attitude; realize that it means you're taking action and are headed toward your goal. Will it always be the most direct route? Probably not, but it means you're headed in the right direction. It means you're Zig Zagging forward.

Focus on Activities

Another problem with traditional goal setting is that it gets you focused completely on the outcome. At the beginning of this chapter, you heard Chris's original goal of "making $100,000 a year by graduation to avoid getting a job" and how he broke down that goal into making $20,000 the first year, $50,000 the second, and $100,000 the third year. The instant he didn't make his goal of $20,000 (the outcome) the first year, he was already failing at his goal and starting toward the "downward spiral."

Rather than focusing on the outcome, it's best to focus on activities that will lead toward your goal. We say to focus on activities rather than the outcome because you have control over the activities that you do on a regular basis, but not always over the outcome. It's impossible to achieve the outcome you want without putting in the activities needed to get there. This statement may seem like common sense, yet most traditional goal setting plans overlook this basic common sense rule. Once Chris realized that he needed to focus on activities, he changed his whole approach to setting and achieving goals. To the best of his abilities, he figured out what activities he needed to do on a regular basis in order to reach his goal of $100,000 a year by graduation. As his business grew, he learned more and made adjustments, and the activities changed with those adjustments. Many of the typical activities included creating websites, working on marketing pieces, recording and listening to himself to improve his communication skills, following-up with customers or potential customers, working on his mindset daily, and doing other activities necessary to becoming an Anti Suit Entrepreneur.

Activities are something that can be crossed or checked off your to-do list. Think about the satisfaction and sense of accomplishment you get when you're able to check off a lot of items from your to-do list. It makes most people happier and more organized and gets them setup for accomplishing more things done down the road. The same is true as you check off activities for working toward your goals. Getting more activities accomplished and checked off causes an "upward spiral of success." This success gets you into the zone or flow, boosts your self confidence, and helps you accomplish more the following week. It has a compounding effect on creating an even more powerful "upward spiral of success."

Focusing on activities rather than outcomes also forces you to figure out what the heck you need to do in order to accomplish your goals! After a couple of months of saying affirmations and reading his goals on daily basis, Chris started doubting himself because he wasn't actually doing anything and had no clue what he needed to do to make a $100,000 per year! You can only fool yourself so long before reality sets in. Determining the activities that you need to do in order to get to a goal actually forces you to create your game plan. Is determining the activities a piece of cake? No. But, if you want to achieve your goal, you're going to have to figure out your activities, sooner or later. Working with a mentor and being plugged into a community help greatly in meeting this challenge.

Zig Zagging Toward Your Goal

Step #1: Set your goal. You still set your goal as you would under any goal setting plan. You still need to determine your end point or desired outcome. You need to know what you're working toward. How you set your goal and stay focused are up to you and your personality. A very popular method is creating a dream board. Traditionally, to create a dream board, you get a big piece of poster board, cut out pictures from magazines, and glue them to the poster board. You get photos and pictures of what you want and what your goal will realistically allow. You then position the board somewhere that you'll see it often, perhaps, in your home office, to constantly remind you of your goal.

We do our dream boards a little differently. Rather than using poster board and magazine photos, we've created background images or wall paper for our computer desktops. Most image editing softwares will allow you to do this. We typically do ours with Keynote, which is Apple's version of PowerPoint. The software is very easy to use and allows us to quickly make the wallpaper and post it on our desktop, so we see it constantly.

Is one method better than the other? No. The best method is whatever works best for you. Just make sure you set your goal!

Step #2: Create an activity focused action plan. You will need to figure out what activities will bring you a step closer to your goal. Remember, an activity is an actionable item that you can cross off your to-do list. You won't be able, on day one, to make a list of every single activity that you need to do in order to achieve your goal. It's impossible to do. Rather, create a list of the activities that you need to do to get you moving toward your goal. Some of these activities will be one time things, others will be ones that you do on a recurring basis. In fact, once you get up and running toward your goal, most of your activities will be recurring ones.

Many of our businesses rely on our Internet marketing Money Making Skills to generate new customers and stay in touch with our current ones. We've been marketing on the Internet for so many years now that we know the recipe for creating a successful website that leads to increased business. We schedule recurring activities for each business around writing newsletters, recording and uploading videos, writing blog entries, posting to Facebook, and managing our online advertisements. Doing those activities on a consistent and recurring basis always leads us to more customers and more business! Growing our customer base and our income is a step in the right direction toward our goals.

Step #3: Just start taking action. Once you come up with your initial set of necessary activities, just start taking action and crossing them off! This step is so important in developing the Anti Suit Entrepreneur mindset. You need to get into action and start working toward your goals. Don't wait for the stars to align or the timing to be perfect because it never will be.

Step #4: Keep zig zagging forward. No matter what! Life is going to throw you curve balls. You will have "sh*t happens" moments. You will hit dead ends as you go through the maze. You will take two steps forward, one step back as you try to achieve your goals. You need to wrap your head around this. This is a big paradigm shift because we're taught that any failure is bad. But, it's not. This idea may sound weird, but you need to embrace all of these things. Those things happening means that you're on the right track and working toward your goal.

Staying On Track

Understand that dealing with all the curve balls that life throws at you is easier said than done. We have figured out a very good method for helping us get back on track.

Tip #1: Realize how far you've come. Chris enjoys hiking and backpacking and relates this idea to hiking up a mountain. While you're hiking up, it can seem as though you're getting nowhere. The trail seems to never endsand is always going up and up. The longer you go the more out of breath you get and the more your legs burn. It can seem as though you will never reach your goal of getting to the top. But when you stop and look at how far you've climbed up the mountain, you realize just how far you have come. It seems that we always focus on what's ahead and how much we have left to go, not on how much we've accomplished. You need to retrain yourself to take breaks to see just how far you've come.

Tip #2: Put things into perspective relative to how far you've actually come. As Chris was working toward his "$100,000 a year by graduation" goal, he became frustrated when he didn't achieve his first goal of $20,000 a year. He didn't make $20,000, but he made close to $10,000. Once he put making $10,000 as an Anti Suit Entrepreneur into perspective, it made him realize how far he had come. The $10,000 in income represented the first money he ever made that wasn't earned from a paycheck by working for someone else. He made the $10,000 on his schedule with the knowledge and skills that he learned recently. He put it into perspective by focusing on what he accomplished, rather than focusing on his perceived failures.

Tip #3: Evaluate your progress and then make adjustments. While he was putting it into perspective, Chris evaluated what went right and what could have gone better and then made adjustments to his future activities. Making a wrong turn in the maze or hitting a dead end are not bad things. They are a learning experience. Do the best you can to learn from your mistakes and avoid repeating the same ones. Also realize that you're gaining invaluable real world experience that you can only get by taking action.

Tip #4: Never stop zig zagging. Never. Once you've realized how far you've come, put things into perspective and made adjustments, get back to zig zagging toward your goal. Don't stop zig zagging until you achieve it. By the time Chris graduated, he did not achieve his full goal of "making $100,000 a year by graduation to avoid getting a job." Chris made just over $50,000 that year in both active and recurring income. However, he was making enough that he didn't have to get a job when he graduated. In fact, he was making more money than many of his peers who graduated and got jobs.

While Chris technically didn't achieve his goal, did he really fail? No. He built up a recurring income that allowed him to live life on his terms and move to South Beach, Miami, FL. He put everything into perspective, made adjustments, and then kept zig zagging on to make a $100,000 a year soon after that.

Being Effective and Efficient

You need to be effective *and* efficient in your goal accomplishing activities in order to achieve those goals. Effective goal accomplishing activities are about producing the desired result with the *right* activities. Efficient goal accomplishing activities are about maximizing your productivity, while minimizing wasted time, effort and money.

You don't want to be efficient for the sake of getting a lot done, if what you're doing is not effective at helping you reach your goal. At the same time, you can't spend forever on one activity getting it just right, when you have dozens or hundreds more to do!

Often times it seems people are either effective *or* efficient, not both. If you want to become an Anti Suit Entrepreneur, then you need to become both efficient and effective. We work by three rules to help us be our most productive, while being both efficient and effective. We have nicknamed these three rules, the Big Three. These rules have helped us tremendously in achieving our goals.

Rule #1: The 80/20 Rule

The 80/20 Rule is popular in the business world. Generally speaking, you can expect 80 percent of your results from 20 percent of your efforts. The converse of 20 percent of results coming from 80 percent of your efforts holds true as well. Many businesses will report that 80 percent of their sales are made by 20 percent of their sales staff, or that 80 percent of their income comes from 20 percent of their customers or a particular product line. In our years of running businesses, we have seen similar patterns.

The 80/20 Rule is something that you want to keep in mind while you're working toward your goals. You want to make sure you're doing the 20 percent of activities that produce 80 percent, or the majority of the results. It's not always a 80/20 relationship. Sometimes it's a 70/30, 90/10, or even a 95/5 relationship! Don't get tunnel vision on always expecting 80 percent of your results coming from 20 percent of your activities. Rather, focus on the patterns that emerge on what is bringing in the most results, whether that is clients, income, or personal satisfaction. When you start observing, you'll notice the 80/20 patterns starting to appear.

We've seen many people whom we've mentored put a lot of time into becoming an Anti Suit Entrepreneur, but produce very little results in actually becoming one. This failure is because they have focused on the 80 percent of activities that bring in the 20 percent of minimal results. When we see people put in time, but not getting results, we have them do an exercise where they set a timer to go off every 15 minutes. Every time the timer goes off, they jot down what they've been doing for the last 15 minutes. This exercise is tedious, but it's also very eye opening. Many people are amazed at how much time they are wasting on nonproductive activities. Organizing your desk and cleaning your home office are nice, but they are not going to increase your income.

As you're working toward your goals, ask yourself if you're doing the activities that will get you the greatest results. This questioning is very similar to the ROLIFE concept, except it's on an activity by activity basis. Is there a better activity you can do to achieve more results or give you a better return on your effort? If there is, you need to rethink what you're doing.

Rule #2: The KISS Principle

We are huge fans of the Keep It Simple, Silly (KISS) principle. It's very easy to overcomplicate projects and activities. We each work on different projects and different parts of our businesses. We're constantly in touch with each other's work so there's a second set of eyes looking it over. Sometimes one of us will see something that is more complicated than it needs to be. When that happens, we let the other person know. We have found that the simpler we keep things, the more money we make with fewer headaches.

Constantly ask yourself, "Is there a simpler way to do this?" and "Am I over complicating this?" It's very easy to get tunnel vision or miss simple solutions when you're working by yourself. This is another reason we're so adamant about working with mentors and being plugged into a community because you'll have a second set of eyes looking at what you're doing.

Rule #3: Brain Dump on a Regular Basis

At some point, you'll get confused or overwhelmed as you're trying to achieve a goal. When you're spinning your wheels, not making as much progress as you'd like, or feeling overwhelmed, then do a brain dump. A brain dump is simply writing down every single thing that you need to get done and that is on your mind. Write down everything that is big and small in all areas of your life and business. If one part of your life is chaotic, it's going to affect the other areas.

Dumping all the information from your brain is going to allow you to relax and then get organized. Once everything is out of your brain, go about organizing the information. The key here is to make everything into an individual action item that can be checked off your to-do list. An individual action item is something that you can accomplish independent of anything else, for example, paying your car insurance. If you have something that has multiple steps to it, then you need to break it down into individual action items. This process could range from a couple of individual action steps to hundreds of individual action steps.

Typically, when we tell people to break down all their projects in this method, we hear back, "That sounds like too much work" or "I don't have the time do that." Once they do a brain dump and organize everything, they tell us how helpful it was! Most importantly, we start seeing them getting more done and having more success.

We routinely do this ourselves and have the people we're mentoring do this, too. Every time we do it, we feel less stress and more relaxed. Since our brain isn't juggling 50 different things, our creativity, focus, and productivity go up. Make sure you keep the 80/20 rule and KISS principle in mind as you're doing your brain dump!

Just Keep Zig Zagging, No Matter What

The biggest thing to take away from this chapter is the necessity to keep zig zagging, no matter what. Taking action will always take you a step closer to your goal. We would not be where we are today, if we didn't just keep zig zagging through our failures and through life's curve balls. Since we have, we've accomplished an incredible amount. So much so, that our friends and people we mentor often comment on how much that we have achieved. We don't share that information to brag, but to let you know how important zig zagging toward your goals is. Far too often we've seen people who have great progress in their Anti Suit Entrepreneurial journey, and then give up when they were so close to achieving their goals. You will get frustrated. You will hit road blocks. Life will throw you curve balls. But, that's how it is for everyone! The people who make it are the ones that keep zig zagging.

We know, if you follow this advice, you'll be amazed at how much you accomplish. It may not happen the way you expected it to, but it'll happen. Remember, just keep zig zagging, no matter what.

CHARGE AHEAD
HOMEWORK

Get it. Read it. **Apply it.**

We have put together a logical, simple sheet that we personally use to accomplish things. Use it as a reference to help you stay productive as you zig zag toward your goals. Download the Goal Setting Cheat Sheet at www.AntiSuitEntrepreneur.com/chapter9

Chapter 10
Whoever Has the Biggest Rolodex Wins

Forget, "Who do you know?" It's all about, "Who do you have relationships with?"

Now, we don't actually keep a rolodex on our desks (don't think too many people do anymore). But we like the visual image it offers. It represents people whom you can call up and say, "Hey {name}, this is {your name}..." and the person instantly recognizes your name and voice and then is happy starting a conversation with you because you two have a solid relationship established.

Even though the world is becoming more digital with social media websites, the importance and power of authentic relationships are growing because more and more people have surface relationships. An authentic relationship is one in which you can talk with a person and have a meaningful conversation about life, business, sharing ideas, or just catching up. A surface relationship is one in which two people know each other, but there is no substance in the relationship because neither really knows the other one. We call them surface relationships because there is no depth to the relationship.

Social media and text messaging are drivers behind people having more surface relationships than authentic relationships. Just think how often you see a group of people at a restaurant or coffee shop, where everyone is sitting around the table texting away on their smartphones and barely having conversations with others at the table. Or think about how many people have thousands of social media friends and followers, but very few real friends because they spend all their time seeing and commenting on what other people are doing.

Don't get us wrong, we use social media and are guilty of sometimes sitting around the dinner table texting on our phones, while neglecting the person sitting two feet from us. However, we make it a point to develop and maintain authentic relationships. While we probably have fewer Facebook friends than most people, we have a rolodex that includes Olympic medalists, millionaires, mega successful real estate investors, executives at corporations listed on the NYSE and NASDAQ, and hundreds of other like-minded people. More importantly, we have authentic relationships with these people.

The More Authentic Relationships You Have, The More Opportunities You Will Have

It's important to have authentic relationships because the more you have, the more opportunities you will have. We don't just mean entrepreneurial and money making related opportunities, but also opportunities to live a happier and more fulfilling life. When you have authentic relationships with people who have similar interests, you'll develop a friendship through which you can pursue the common interest together. Or those people will share new ideas with you, exposing you to new areas of life that you haven't explored yet. Some of these relationships will develop into great friendships. Generally, the more friends you have, the happier you are.

Every year Chris tries to go on an "off the grid" outdoor trip with a group of friends from college. The goal of the trip is to completely disconnect from the world, be self reliant, and explore a new part of the world. One trip Chris and his friends took was to a remote part of Canada to go canoeing for the week. In order to get there, they chartered a water plane to drop them, their canoes, and their gear off in the middle of a lake. For the next week, they paddled through a series of connected lakes and rivers to a predetermined point where the water plane would pick them up to take them back to civilization. There were numerous white water rapids run and there were ones that were too dangerous and big to run, so Chris and his friends portaged the rapids to go around. They went days without seeing anyone else and only had a satellite phone to use in an emergency and would have to wait a minimum of 24 hours before any plane or helicopter could reach them. They were on their own with no guide, outfitter, or other people around, and that's exactly how they wanted it.

We wanted to preface the common business saying of "People do business with people they know, like and trust" with Chris's canoe trip story. It was an incredible trip of a lifetime, but also one that posed risks because of the remoteness. No one would have gone on the trip with the others if they didn't trust each other 100% to help out in a potential life threatening emergency. On a different note, the trip wouldn't have happened if the four people didn't like each other, since they would spending so much time together! Chris and his friends all have authentic relationships with each other, in which they "know, like, and trust" each other on a very high level.

Now, one doesn't need the level of "know, like, and trust" that Chris and his friends have, in order to do business, but there needs to be at least some level. Just as Chris and his friends would not go on trips together if they didn't "know, like, and trust" each other, the majority of successful, smart, and savvy people will not do business, make a connection with, or invest in someone they do not "know, like, and trust." People don't want to put their reputation or bank account on the line with just anyone!

You get people to "know, like, and trust" you by building authentic relationships. You build new authentic relationships by building up your rolodex. Building a big rolodex full of people with whom we have authentic relationships, has helped us live life on our terms from both a business and personal standpoint. The majority of our cash flow has come from people in our rolodex who "know, like, and trust" us.

You'll even have some authentic relationships that add to your personal and business life. When we decided to learn FX (currency exchange market) trading, we made it a goal to develop relationships with people who were successful traders. Through building our rolodex, we developed an authentic relationship with a very successful FX trader who lived in Greece. Within a few months of developing that relationship, we were in Greece, watching and learning how he traded FX, while also exploring a new country. Many of our friends shook their heads in disbelief that we were able to build an authentic business relationship long distance, and then actually have the time and money available to fly over there. We were able to do that because we had developed the Anti Suit Entrepreneur lifestyle.

The FX trader also lived the Anti Suit Entrepreneur lifestyle. We would spend a few hours a day trading and learning and then the rest of the day having fun and exploring Greece. Jason and the FX trader both shared a common interest in music and DJing. That interest led to them building an even stronger relationship on a personal level that eventually led to Jason flying back a few months later to attend a music festival that the FX trader was helping to coordinate.

When you stop and think about all of that, it's pretty amazing. We've had other relationships lead to adventures that developed into new businesses and new friendships. Learning how to build our rolodexes has helped us increase our ROLIFE.

Learn How To Build Your Rolodex

Networking is the common word used in the business world when people discuss meeting new people in order to build relationships. The Merriam-Webster Dictionary's definition of networking is "the cultivation of productive relationships for employment or business." We don't like the idea of meeting people just so you can get something out of the relationship in order to increase your income. Many people have expressed similar feelings.

Another reason we don't like the idea of networking is that the concept of networking typically focuses on the *where to go* rather than the *how to build relationships*. Learning the *how to build relationships* is much more important than the *where to go* aspects. Networking usually gets people boxed into a mindset where they can only meet people and establish relationships at networking events. That's just not true! There is no magical or perfect spot for networking because everywhere you go is an opportunity to meet a new person and potentially build a new relationship.

Networking brings along the connotations of building relationships only to increase your income and to exclusively meet people at networking events. These negative aspects are why we refer to building new relationships as building your rolodex and not networking. We've each developed authentic relationships in different situations and settings, such as the yoga studio, the gym, social settings, and over the Internet. Once you learn how to build relationships, then you can do it anywhere, whether it's face to face or using social media and the Internet.

In order to build your rolodex and relationships, you must be a good communicator. We may sound like a broken record because we keep referring to the importance of communication is, but it's worth the effort! Learning how to communicate effectively is a very important Money Making Skill that is the foundation for building your rolodex.

Don't Be A Bad Communicator

The rest of this chapter will focus on helping you become a better communicator so you can build your rolodex. The easiest way to become a better communicator is to learn what not to do in order to avoid being a bad communicator.

You want to make sure you avoid what we call the telemarketer syndrome, where you only talk about yourself and your interests, no matter what the person says. We've all had telemarketers call us, who are reading scripts and seem determined to get through the script as fast as possible. In a face to face situation, people are not as bad as telemarketers. However, it's a very common rookie mistake to have the telemarketer syndrome by only talking about yourself and your interests. Having told 10 people what you do for work may sound okay, yet if you didn't establish some form of a relationship, you probably won't hear from any of those people. You definitely do not want to be that person who never shuts up, whom people try to avoid at all costs. That's not good for business. You'd be better off talking to no one!

When Chris started building his rolodex, he would say to himself, "I know a lot about myself, but nothing about the person with whom I'm talking. Rather than me talking about myself, I'm going to focus on learning about this person." This plan helped Chris avoid the telemarketer syndrome and allowed him to do what great communicators do: actively listening to the other person.

You've probably heard the saying, "We have two ears and one mouth so that we can listen twice as much as we speak." There is truth to that and it's a very good rule of thumb. However, active listening involves much more than just shutting up and listening to the person speak. One part of active listening is asking questions to dig deeper into what the person is talking about. Asking questions will provide you a richer, more meaningful conversation because you're really understanding what the person is saying. If you're asking questions to learn more about the person, he is going to appreciate it and your interest. How often do people take the time to listen to someone and learn more about him? Not very often because it's incredibly rare for someone to take the time to show interest in another person.

If you're not sure what questions to ask, then you're not really listening to the person. Whenever we talk with someone, there are always questions to ask based on what the person is saying. Don't get worried about asking the perfect set of questions because there isn't one. Remember to take the mindset that you're learning about a new person and a new topic, so you want to ask questions along those lines. As you're asking questions, make sure you don't take it too far and turn it into a job interview, where you're just asking question after question without adding anything to the conversation.

Another aspect of active listening is to make sure you're actually listening to the person and not being distracted by your own thoughts, your cell phone, or other things around you. Not being distracted is the number one thing that will make asking questions easier because if you're actually listening to the person, you'll know what they are talking about and will be able to ask relevant questions. Not being distracted may seem as if it's common sense, but it's easier said than done. Have you ever been talking with someone who asks you a question or says something, but have no idea what he is talking about because you got distracted and zoned out? Yes, it's a little embarrassing. It's also rude because it's basically showing the person that whatever you were distracted by is more important than he is.

We're all humans and we're going to get distracted and zoned out. So, when you do get distracted by someone walking by or a thought pops in your mind and you miss what the person said, just be honest and tell the person you got distracted. He'll understand (he's human, too!) and will most likely appreciate you telling him so. Just don't try to act like you were listening, when you weren't. That deception will just snowball into a bigger and more embarrassing situation.

Our Communication Process

In most of our businesses, we have to train people how to communicate. We use a very simple but effective communication process that is effective and easy to teach. We want to share that process with you. Understand that we could write a whole book on this topic; it will be challenging for us to condense this information and still show you the process in a few pages. We wanted to give you at least a small foundation from which to work.

One of the first questions we get from people is, "Why do I need to treat communication as a process?" The answer is that having a process gives you direction to help you build relationships. It's also helpful to diagnose any potential issues you have as you communicate with people.

Connect

The first step in effective communication is connecting with someone. This step is fairly simple because you cannot build relationships if you don't meet new people. Anytime you meet or talk with a new person, you're in the Connect step. You're probably connecting with new people every single day. If you want to build your rolodex, you need to put yourself in situations where you can meet new people in order to make connections. It's that simple.

Develop

The second step in the process is developing the relationship. In this step, you actively engage the person so you can start building an authentic relationship. This step can take minutes, hours, days, months, or years. There is no good or bad amount of time. How long it takes depends on many factors. The Develop step is where you really begin to get to know the person.

When we're in the Develop step, we ask ourselves these questions:

Question #1 - Do you even like the person? If you don't like a person or enjoy a person's company, then don't bother with continuing the relationship. Even if there is potential for doing business together, we will stop building the relationship if we don't like the person. It's hard to live life on your terms if you've surrounded yourself with people you don't like!

Question #2 - Is it realistic that we will continue to build a relationship with this person? Even if we enjoy the person's company, we may not continue building the relationship for a variety of reasons.

Question #3 - Is the person a friend, potential partner in business, or potentially both?

Our method of building relationships is to go through our rolodex until we make two meaningful connections a day. What is a meaningful connection? It's a conversation that is substantive enough that it adds to the relationship. Depending on your relationship with the person, this could be a phone call, a text message, a social media message, getting together for coffee, or any method that allows you to actually talk with the person.

We make it a goal to have two meaningful conversations a day in order to build and maintain relationships. Sometimes you have to dial two phone numbers; sometimes you need to dial twenty numbers. If you want to build relationships with people, you need to want to talk to them, build a relationship with them, and therefore take the time to reach out to them. Remember what they say about relationships between a man and woman: "They take work." It's not that husband/wife or boyfriend/girlfriend relationships take work. It's that *all* relationships take work. That is why our first question we ask ourselves before we enter a contact is: "Do we like this person?" If you build a relationship with someone you don't like, then you are just setting yourself to *not* live life on your terms.

We can hear the concerns now: "But Jason, Chris, calling your rolodex until you get two people seems so structured and unnatural." It might be at first. But whenever you think that, remember that relationships take work and if you don't carve out the time for those relationships, you won't work on them. It's that simple. You have to make it a daily activity goal until it becomes natural to you.

Introduce

This step is reserved for those times when someone in your rolodex may be a fit for a project you are working on. It could be having the person be an investor, a mentor, partnering with you, or even becoming a client. If you want to discuss a potential project, idea, or whatever that can take you and them to the next level, then this is where this step takes control.

People will not reach this step in the communication process unless a person "is a fit" for the situation at hand. Basically the way this happens is when something comes up, a certain person will pop into your mind, and it will be time for you to Introduce your project to them.

An example of this step is building communities. Later in this book, we discuss the importance of building strong Anti Suit Entrepreneur communities around you, and we go into some detail on how to do it, and on what skills you need to do to accomplish that. Maybe as you're building your future Anti Suit Entrepreneur community, a person in your rolodex comes to mind. You think "they would be great for my Anti Suit Entrepreneur community." When you discussed what you were doing with them, that would be the Introduce step.

The Introduce step isn't just for business related things. It's also for personal things as well. Chris's friend organized the canoe trip to Canada and had to introduce the idea to the group and get them all on board with the idea.

Follow-Up

If you have read any type of sales book, then you have heard about the Follow-Up step. This is probably the most universal step in any sales or communication process. If you don't follow-up, then typically the Introduce step doesn't move forward. You, we, and everyone out there have fifty or more things going on at once. If you don't follow-up with someone, then what you Introduced will get lost in the shuffle of life.

Frankly, we can write a whole book on this part of the communication process alone, but sharing a story is probably the best way to show the importance of Follow-up.

In one of Jason's businesses, he had Connected and Developed a gentleman. Eventually there was a business project that Jason Introduced to this person. After Introducing the project, he followed-up by phone (and confirmation email) five times, without hearing anything back from the gentleman. On the fifth call, Jason left a voicemail saying, "I am assuming you're not interested at this point in the project that we discussed. I have to move on. Good luck to you." Shortly after that message, the gentleman called Jason back and partnered with him on the project. With this person on board, it ended up being incredibly lucrative for both of them.

What if Jason wouldn't have followed-up with this person? Follow-up is important in any relationship, especially if you have reached the Introduce step. When a relationship progresses to this point (often times it's business), you need to act in a professional manner and people expect you to follow-up. It's that simple. The gentleman actually said that he was "testing" Jason to see if he had what it takes. He was impressed with Jason's follow-up and that's why he ended up working with him. How many successful people have you passed up on because you didn't do the Follow-up step?

Close

In the Close step, you get all the final questions answered and details figured out between you and the person with whom you're talking, to determine if he's on board or not with your Introduce project. If you don't present the option or ask the person if he is ready to move forward, you'll never start the project! Very few people will call you up and tell you that they are ready to go. That's why you need to get with the person and come to a conclusion as to whether or not you're going to move forward.

Sometimes the Close step makes a person recall past experiences of salespeople trying to convince him or do a "hard close" in order to sell something. That's not what we want or intend to do to people. Our philosophy is to Follow-up with the person until we can come to a decision point. Of course, we'd always like every single person to say, "Yes," but that's not realistic. We just want to know what decision the person is making, so both parties can move forward, whether that's working together or not. Getting closure and a decision are what is important to us, so we can continue the relationship. Even if a person says, "No" to one of our business ideas, we don't remove him from our rolodex. We continue to stay in touch, to maintain the relationship, because you never know where that might lead.

Your Inner Circle

As you grow your rolodex, you will begin to build a select group of people with whom you are very close. These people will play a big role in your success. We wouldn't be where we are today without these people.

Years ago, we were building our rolodex by making our connections and developing our relationships, which led us to a person who became critical to some of our businesses. Many of our businesses are built around technology, so having someone competent at computer programming, web programming, and other programming languages was critical. We had the "know-how" and "processes," but we needed someone to put that into systems. We met a gentleman who was a computer programmer with 20 years consulting and corporate experience with a degree in Computer Science and an MBA. He used to build systems for the commodity exchanges out of Chicago. He was a solid guy with a great skill set when it came to programming languages and technology. Like us, he was an entrepreneur at heart and was tired of dealing with unreasonable corporate people and consulting clients.

Jason Introduced an idea about working together in some businesses. Wall ended up working together and it created a win-win situation. Because of the knowledge and skill sets he brought to the table, he and Jason were able to work together in building a very robust marketing system. When people with programming backgrounds find out that our system was built by only two people, they are blown away.

The point is we may never have met this guy if we weren't building our rolodex. He was one of the people in our rolodex who became an Inner Circle person for us, ultimately partnered in projects with us, and also became a good friend. Hopefully, you can see the value of building your rolodex and developing your Inner Circle.

To emphasize our point: you never know where a relationship can lead. You never know what a person will become to you personally or professionally; therefore, the more people you add to your rolodex, the better. So, no matter where you are in your entrepreneurial journey, start building your rolodex.

ANTI SUIT
CHARGE AHEAD
HOMEWORK

Get it. Read it. **Apply it.**

Communication is the most important skill you can learn in becoming an entrepreneur. Get started on the "right foot" by following our communication process that we use in our businesses as well as our daily lives. Download our Communication Cheat Sheet from the website at www.AntiSuitEntrepreneur.com/chapter10

Chapter 11
Communities Get More Done

Communities are often associated with churches, neighborhoods, and schools, but are not often associated with entrepreneurship and business, which is unfortunate because they can be extremely powerful in helping you becoming an Anti Suit Entrepreneur. We learned the importance and power of entrepreneurial focused communities inadvertently from one of our first business projects.

As with all businesses, Jason experienced growing pains in one of his businesses due to its fast growth, which is a great problem to have. From running and expanding the law firm, he knew that utilizing technology and systems were critical for the long term health of a business. He searched for software solutions, but couldn't find any to fit the needs of his new business. There were many systems available, but trying to make them fit his business needs would have been like trying to fit a square peg in a round hole. In chapter 2, *The New College Degree,* we told the story of how Jason taught himself the Money Making Skill of computer programming. So he decided to build his own system from the ground up, to meet the needs of his business. The new system helped his business tremendously, to say the least.

People in Jason's Inner Circle and rolodex noticed Jason's success with his new system. They started asking questions about it and then started asking Jason if they could use the system as well. Some were very eager and practically beating down his door to use it! As far as we know, Jason's system was one of the first systems designed for the Anti Suit Entrepreneurial type. All the systems available then were geared toward corporate clients, not individual entrepreneurs conducting the majority of their business over the Internet. Jason never intended to let other people use his system, but as he thought about it, he realized it was a win-win for everyone. It could help other Anti Suit Entrepreneurs with their businesses and also provide cash flow to maintain the system and expand it, to have its own programming staff one day.

At this point, Jason had been Chris's Vested Mentor for a while. Jason decided to bring Chris on board to help out with the system, since a good working relationship had been established. Jason bringing Chris on board is just one example of why having Vested Mentors can be important for you. You never know what new doors the mentor relationships may open up.

Jason added a message board and email list to the system, so people could ask technical questions on using it. Over the months, we started seeing people posting marketing and business specific questions and ideas to get feedback from other entrepreneurs. It got to the point where more people were posting questions regarding their own business than how-to system questions! All the ideas being shared helped many people grow their own businesses. We started hearing stories how people were forming mastermind groups to hold each other accountable and even partnering together to help one another out in their businesses.

As ideas were shared and people's businesses grew, we saw massive jumps in new entrepreneurs joining and using the system, which was an unexpected surprise. Chris spoke with many of the new entrepreneurs joining the system and asked them why they joined. Their responses revealed two common themes. One theme was that they needed a system to help them with their business. The other theme was that they wanted to be connected with other like-minded entrepreneurs to share ideas, hold each other accountable, have fun, and just be a part of a group. Many people would tell Chris how their schedules didn't fit with joining local groups in their area or that none of the local groups had entrepreneurs who were conducting the business on the Internet the way we were.

One person described feeling as if he were on an island because he had no fellow entrepreneurs with whom to build camaraderie. That's when the power and importance of having an entrepreneurial focused community dawned on us. All throughout history, people from every civilization formed communities for safety, social, economic, and quality of life reasons. Entrepreneurs using the Internet were starving to be part of an entrepreneurial focused community.

When Jason started this system, the Internet was a very different landscape. It was still in its infancy. The Internet opened up unprecedented opportunities for growing and running a business. The ability to run a business from home or any location brought about a whole new breed of entrepreneurs. It had many of these entrepreneurs excited about the potential, but confused on how to make everything work together. Keep in mind that social media was almost nonexistent at the time. Social media was not part of a person's day to day life as it is now. The first version of Jason's system was created even before MySpace (if you even remember that social media platform) was founded in August 2003. That should help put things into perspective on just how ahead of its time Jason's system was. It should also put the landscape into perspective about how it was nearly impossible for like-minded entrepreneurs to connect with each other back then.

The majority of our members are based in the U.S. and Canada, but we also have people from all around the world using our system. Many of these people were on "islands by themselves," as they sat behind their computer in their home office. Together, they end up forming an international community of entrepreneurs sharing ideas and building camaraderie with each other. It's impossible for us to measure and calculate a statistic on the impact that the community has had on people's businesses. However, over the years, we've had hundreds of people tell us how much the community aspect of our system helped them in their business.

Over the last 10 years, our system has gone through numerous updates and new versions as technology has evolved, but the community aspect is still all about connecting like-minded entrepreneurs. Something we've learned over the last decade is that no matter how much technology changes or automates certain aspects of conducing business, communities will never be replaced by technology. Technology may, however, change how people connect and build communities; just think about all the different social media platforms that have come and gone in just the last few years. But nothing can compare to a group of like-minded people sharing ideas and building camaraderie.

Communities Are Undervalued

As with all successful products and businesses, others try to copy it. People have tried (and still try) to copy us. The first couple of times it happened, it irritated us because aspects of our system were blatantly copied and some of the copycats even trash talked us and our system. Chris's first thought, as was many people's, was to take them to court and sue them. Chris was surprised when Jason, the person who used to run law firms and had a law degree, said, "No way. I've seen way too many businesses win the battle, but lose the war. Winning the lawsuit (the battle) can take years and have legal fees into the six or even seven figures. The typical outcome is one where the competitor can't even pay any damages. In the long run (the war), the business lost because it can't collect any money, spent a ton of money on legal fees, and spent the last couple of years focusing on the lawsuit rather than the business itself. Besides, if the only way the competitors could make money is by copying someone else, they're going to end up putting themselves out of business eventually."

Jason was correct in his assessment. All the copycats have either crashed and burned or are floundering around.

These copycats focused on specific system features to copy or creating all these fancy bells and whistles. Focusing on those didn't work, because we're constantly innovating, and because they were never able to create a community of like-minded entrepreneurs. Most don't realize the power and importance of a community, when it comes to entrepreneurship. The ones who did and tried to create a community, failed at it. From our perspective, it's obvious why their attempts at creating communities failed: when you copy and trash talk other people, what type of customers do you expect to attract?

Many of the most successful products, brands, and businesses have built amazing communities! Think about some of your most favorite products and services that you use. What types of communities are built around them?

Communities are important because they will help you on your entrepreneurial journey and help you grow your own successful business, regardless of whatever your product or service is. It's hard to put a value on a community and how much it can impact someone's life because it's about people and the connections they make with each other. When like-minded people are together, something almost magical happens. There's synergy among people which creates energy and excitement that gets carried over outside the community and into people's businesses.

Through the community that went along with our system, Chris built a relationship with a fellow entrepreneur. They became good friends. At some point along the way, they decided to form a mastermind group where they would meet on the phone once a week and share successes, problems, and ideas from the recent week. They also would read a chapter each week in a business book and discuss the ideas and how they could apply them to their own business. They met every week for about a year and each received enormous benefit from being in a mastermind group together, even though their businesses did not affect the other's. The mastermind group was an important step for both of them building successful businesses.

Communities are very beneficial when it comes to helping people through the rough spots of entrepreneurship. Many people who want to become an Anti Suit Entrepreneur quit too soon because they get discouraged or hit a few speed bumps. Quite a few people in our community have commented to us that they would have quit pursuing their entrepreneurship goals, if it wasn't for the community. The relationships people form help them stick around long enough to have success. You may be having a horrible week, but another person in the community is having a great week. Perhaps something that person says or does helps to lift your spirits or get you off the emotional roller coaster and back on track. A few weeks later the two roles may be reversed and you're giving help and energy to the other person.

What Makes A Great Community

We have learned a lot over the years about what makes a good community and a not so good community. The following points are some very important ones, but it's not an all inclusive list. Keep these points in mind as you're getting plugged into a community or creating your own.

Finding Like-Minded People

This is probably the most obvious point: a community is a group of people, so you need more than just yourself. Focus on finding the people who share similar interests or goals. Don't worry about how many people a community has or how big it is, rather, worry about the quality of people it has. We'd rather have a dozen like-minded people on the same page, than a hundred people with different interests and goals.

When you have a community of like-minded people, the snowball effect will happen. Imagine taking a small snowball and rolling it from the top of a mountain. It starts out very small, but every time it rolls, it picks up speed and gets a little bigger. Once it gets toward the base of the mountain, it'll be huge. Having a small group of like-minded people together in a community will have the same effect for the community and the individuals involved.

Cut Out The Cancer

It's also important to cut out the wrong type of people from the community ASAP. We call this cutting out the cancer. Cancer cells start out very small in the body. They grow and start multiplying, causing serious health issues. One wrong person in a community can grow into big problems down the road and even ruin the entire community. We're talking about people who are constantly negative, rude, and undermining other people.

You will rarely have these types of people in your community, but you need to make sure to take action when they do appear. We've had thousands of people in various communities and fewer than one percent have been a problem. We always give people the benefit of the doubt, so we follow the "three strikes and you're out" rule. When people do something so egregious, that it makes us think they may be a cancer to the community, we get in touch with them right away. The majority of these people have apologized and become outstanding community members. Most of them are just on low points on the emotional roller coaster of becoming an entrepreneur and just needed some help to get back on track. We never hold that against people because everyone (us included) has experienced those lows. We respect the people who get back on track.

If someone gets all three strikes, then we remove them from the community. We don't keep records or particularly care about remembering those people, but there have probably been a few dozen over the years. This isn't a large number when you consider how many people are in our communities, but if we didn't kick them out, they could have caused serious issues within the community.

Medium to Connect

People in the community must be able to connect, talk, and build relationships with each other. The mediums a community uses will vary from one community to another. Fitness related communities often use the gym or studio and fitness related events in the areas as their main medium. Obviously, people need to be in the same geographic location.

Since many people in our communities are spread across the globe, we utilize technology. As technology changes, so do our mediums. Don't get caught up in the latest and greatest technology. The goal is to make it easy and simple for people to connect, share ideas, and build relationships. That's hard to do if the technology platform is changing every other month.

We also incorporate get-togethers into our ways to help build the community. As far as we're concerned, nothing will ever beat people being in the same room. It doesn't need to be fancy or at a five star resort. The best community building get-togethers often happen over an inexpensive meal, a drink at the bar, or a fun social or athletic activity.

Have Fun!

People want to have fun and enjoy the community. Most people have more than enough stress and seriousness in their lives already from work. They don't want to be part of a community that feels like a second job. We've also seen some people focus too much on having fun to the extent that no one gets anything done. It's important to strike a workable balance in your community.

Leadership

Every community requires at least one leader. Most have numerous ones. Leaders are the ones who bring communities together and keep them functioning correctly. Bad communities lack leadership, good communities have good leadership, and great communities have great leadership. Leaders set the tone of the communities.

There are thousands of books written on leadership and its importance because leadership is one of the most important qualities for success. We debated about writing a chapter focused on just leadership, but decided to discuss it instead in the context of communities. We did this because being a part of a community or creating your own community is one the best ways to become a leader and develop that Money Making Skill.

Don't think you have what it takes to be a leader? Well, we're willing to bet that you do. You become a leader by stepping into bigger and bigger leadership roles. Starting and being an active member in a community is one of the best ways to step into a leadership role. Even if you have zero leadership skills, most leaders are thrilled to have people volunteer to step up and help out. Leadership, like other skills, is one that is learned. It's very easy for leaders to delegate a few aspects of the community to an enthusiastic up-and-coming leader by giving him some guidance and advice. It ends up being a win-win-win situation for the leader, the up-and-coming leader, and the community.

We could easily fill this entire book with leadership advice, but we won't. Almost every person over the years with whom we discussed leadership has read more than enough books and has plenty of knowledge on the matter, that he doesn't need anymore before stepping into a leadership role. Rather, he needs to take action and jump into the deep end of the pool, by stepping up into a leadership role. We're betting that most of the people reading this book are the same way.

Personality Types

Understanding personality types is important in all aspects of working with people, such as building a community, making a deal, building your rolodex, and signing up a client or customer. This understanding will help you in personal relationships as well. We've studied about a dozen different courses and books on understanding personality types. We learned from each one and have incorporated it into our day to day communication with people. Through our own experiences and observations, we've learned a lot about personality types as well. Reading a book on a subject is very different from actually going out and having first-hand experiences.

What follows is the combination of our first-hand experiences and our knowledge learned from various courses and books. With the KISS principle and the 80/20 rule in mind, we'll share with you key information that has helped us tremendously. We will use colors to identify the four main personality types.

Reds

Red personalities are the controllers and drivers. They are typically the CEOs in corporations. They are absolutely sure of themselves and their decisions and don't waiver at all. When they make a decision, it's typically a "done deal." They can sometimes appear to be intimidating, unemotional, and lacking empathy. It may seem that their decisions are emotionally detached, but it's not necessarily the case with Reds.

When dealing with Reds, you need to be aware of their need to be right. They can be a powerful ally in a community because they will get things done and find the straightest road to the end goal. As long as a Red isn't doing something detrimental to the community or lacking integrity in his choices, let him get the job done. If it's getting done correctly, let him do it. Make him feel that he is in control of his decision.

However, if he is making choices that are detrimental to the community, then you need to pull him aside and firmly let him know that what he is doing is not acceptable. Since Reds are direct in their communication, they will want you to be direct to them. The "It's my way or the highway" phrase fits this scenario perfectly. He may not like what you're saying, though, and hit the highway and leave the community. You need to be prepared for that.

As a leader, it is often wise to get these people in the leadership positions. They will get the project done no matter what gets in the way. You just need to make sure you have the confidence to be direct with them when needed.

Greens

Green personalties are the analytical types. They are the accountants, engineers, math majors, and scientists. Everything is methodical, logical, and organized with them. They love lists. It's often hard for them to make a decision because there is so much to analyze before a decision can be made. Often they feel like they need to gather all the information first and analyze it to make sure they are not making a wrong decision. They are tremendous organizers and can often be a great addition to communities when it comes to organizing and planning. They are masters at these skills

One of the challenges of working with Greens is that they can be hard to pin down for a deadline. It's not because they aren't working on the project, it's because there's so much information and it all needs to be analyzed first, before even determining a deadline. Don't be surprised if a Green pushes back a deadline. They aren't doing it to be rude, it's because new information popped up that needs to be reviewed and worked into the solution. They'd rather push a deadline back, so they can get things right, rather than meet the deadline with the wrong solution.

One of the great characteristics of Greens is that once they make up their mind, they will work very hard on whatever it is that needs to get done. Rest assured that once a Green agrees to a project, he will see it through to completion.

Blues

Blue personalities are the "let's get started and worry about the details later!" type. They are great at establishing and building relationships, which makes them the salespeople and the "center of attention" social types. For Greens, the "devil is in the details," but this style drives a Blue nuts. They don't like details. They are dreamers and risk-takers and often act without much analysis. They are also very creative.

If you want to approach a project with a "ready, fire, aim" instead of the typical "ready, aim, fire," then the Blue is the person for that job. They are amazing at building relationships, are often great story tellers, and know a lot of people. Their strength is their relationships and that alone makes them powerful.

Their weaknesses are a general lack of follow-through, lack of organization, and aversion to details. A Green and Blue working together can be like mixing oil and water: they just don't mix! Both can easily frustrate the other one. Blues, who are aware of their weaknesses and allow the other types to handle certain aspects of their project, can achieve a tremendous amount.

As a leader, you want the Blues to build the relationships. You want to listen to their ideas because they will give you a lot. It's your job to take the great ones and put the Greens and Reds into executing these ideas. The Blues will be most motivated when they can be social in their duties and have fun in their work.

Yellows

Yellow personalities are the caring people in the group. They often find it hard to speak their mind because they don't want to offend or hurt people. They love to be a part of communities and teams because they love the togetherness. They are the nurturers in the groups, and most of the time, they just want everyone to be happy.

The Yellows are great in helping the Greens organize, especially in the community and team aspects. They will give you great insight into emotionally connecting with people.

Having success in selling an idea and in executing a community or team project highly depends on how people feel about that community. The Yellows can be of help with that. They can create a community that "touches" people in a way that makes them want to be involved, whether or not it makes money for them in the long run.

A weakness of Yellows is that they are easily steam rolled, especially by Reds, since they are not as vocal when it comes to speaking their minds. This situation can cause the community to lose out on great ideas and even have Yellows pull back from the group because their feelings are hurt.

Understanding Personality Types

A popular question is, "What's the best personality type?" There isn't one. No personality type is better than another one. They all have their strengths and weaknesses. All are needed to make the world go around and get projects done.

Another popular question is, "What's my personality type?" Helping you determine that is out of the scope of this book. There are may questionnaires that can help you determine your personality types. We highly recommend you figure out what your type is to give you more insight into your own strengths and weaknesses. However, once you learn it, don't let the label of your personality type box you in and potentially hold you back. No quiz or questionnaire is perfect.

Most people are usually a combination of two colors or two main personality types. In fact, we cannot think of a single person who is only one color and none of the others. Generally a person will predominately be one color with another color as their secondary personality characteristics.

Start trying to identify people's personality types. Notice how they make decisions and how they go about getting projects done. Learning personality types will help you in all areas of your life, not just your entrepreneurial journey. Observing people and what they do is the best way to learn the different personality types.

Finding Your Community

Finding a community with like-minded entrepreneurs will pay dividends when it comes to living life on your terms. Where do you start? First, understand that just because it's an entrepreneurial focused community, doesn't mean that it'll be the right fit for you. There are numerous entrepreneurial communities, so find one that is a fit for you. You can also join more than one community, so you don't need to box yourself into just one. Just don't get spread too thin, where you're a part of numerous communities but are not active in any of them.

Start talking with people in your rolodex. When Chris started his entrepreneurial journey he was surprised at how many of his friends had an interest in entrepreneurship as well. As with Chris, you may be very surprised to learn what your friends and acquaintances are interested in or even working on. If someone recommends a business or entrepreneurship related book, movie, or website to you, make sure you talk with that person because that's a sign he has interests similar to yours.

We also invite you to plug into the Anti Suit Entrepreneur community. One of our goals in publishing this book is to create a well connected community that consists of like-minded people who are currently entrepreneurs or are aspiring entrepreneurs. Very few people understand the power of a community as much as we do. We want to create a powerful community where people can share ideas, build relationships, and support each other in order to help people become successful entrepreneurs. This community building will help all involved reach their next set of entrepreneurial goals.

Starting to create your own Anti Suit Entrepreneur community will help you develop your leadership skills, become a better communicator, and build your rolodex. It may be overwhelming to some readers, but starting your own community will have a huge impact on your entrepreneurial journey, just as it did for us. Use knowledge from this book and our Anti Suit Entrepreneur community to help you get started.

ANTI SUIT
CHARGE AHEAD
HOMEWORK

Get it. Read it. **Apply it.**

You will get more done with a community around you. It's more fun, you build relationships, and you have more brains from which to pull ideas in your Anti-Suit Entrepreneur quest. Build your own Anti Suit Entrepreneur community at www.AntiSuitEntrepreneur.com/chapter11

Chapter 12
Living Life on Your Terms is a Choice

Living Life on Your Terms is a Choice. We wanted to start this chapter by writing the title again to drive home its importance. What do we mean by "Living Life on Your Terms" is a choice? Think back about our discussion in Chapter 1 about "First World Problems." When you have shelter, food, and your health, people often get complacent. This complacency leads people to "not getting it done" when it comes to your Anti Suit Entrepreneur journey. It's a choice. It's completely up to you. No one is going to make you do what it takes, learn the skills you need to learn, and take action on what you learn. It's completely up to you.

Where to Start

A very common question is, "Where do I start?" We have debated what the best starting point is for a person looking to become an Anti Suit Entrepreneur. We've concluded that it's finding a Vested Mentor. This is a general rule of thumb because your situation may be different, depending on where you are in life and whom you know. However, generally speaking, finding a Vested Mentor is the best first step to take. That step is exactly what Chris did, and it paid off big time.

In 2003 Chris made the decision that he would not take the traditional path of getting a college degree and relying on a job for the rest of his life. He didn't have a clue as to how to go about doing that, but he had the desire. At the time, Chris had no concept of Vested Mentorship, but he knew he needed someone who could teach him business skills. He started searching for that person. Through a very round about way, he connected with Jason and formed a Vested Mentor Relationship. Jason was already on his way to becoming an Anti Suit Entrepreneur and living life on his terms. Chris saw Jason's successes and realized that he could learn a lot from him. And learn a lot he did.

Within a couple of years of starting down the Anti Suit Entrepreneur path and having Jason as a Vested Mentor,

Chris had built enough recurring income that when he graduated Virginia Tech in 2005, he didn't have to get a job. The Vested Mentorship relationship eventually turned into us becoming business partners in a couple of businesses. We'll repeat that: *the Vested Mentorship, that Chris established with Jason, eventually led us to becoming business partners* and increased both of our Diversified Cash Flows.

Our story is a perfect example of how powerful Vested Mentorship really can be. Within a few years of graduating, Vested Mentorship led Chris to living the Anti Suit Entrepreneur lifestyle with Diversified Cash Flow from different businesses. From Jason's perspective, he developed a relationship with someone whom he trusted and who could get things done. Believe it or not, there are many successful people, who have an extremely hard time finding trustworthy and capable people with whom to partner. Successful people are not going to hand you equity in their business or bend over backwards to teach you everything that you need to know. But if you find a Vested Mentor and prove yourself, you never know what could develop. Chris didn't know how things might end, but he worked and searched and achieved success. Often times building a relationship and proving yourself through a Vested Mentorship relationship is the way to go. Our story of becoming business partners via vested mentorship is not unique nor uncommon.

Achieve Your Goals Faster

A vested mentor can help you achieve your goals much faster than if you're just working on your own. Generally, we have found that people who are willing to learn, willing to listen, and willing to follow a plan are able to reduce the time it takes them to achieve their goals. The learning time is cut down because we are able to tell people exactly what they need to learn, help them avoid the mistakes we made, and keep them on track as they "zig-zag" their way to the Anti Suit Entrepreneur lifestyle.

Does getting a Vested Mentor guarantee your success or a quicker route to becoming an Anti Suit Entrepreneur? No, it doesn't. You still need to bring the desire and willingness to work hard. You also need to be teachable or coachable. Over the years, we've had quite a few Vested Mentor relationships with people who were smart and willing to work hard, but weren't coachable. We would provide them guidance and insight into what we've done over the years, but they didn't implement our advice. It's very frustrating, from our point of view, because we know they could be so much farther along. Some people don't listen because they have an ego. Other people, and this is the majority of non-coachable people, don't realize that they are being bull-headed and non-coachable.

In one of our businesses, we earn a substantial monthly recurring income. Some of the people we are mentoring are making nothing or a few hundred dollars a month in a similar business. Yet, they try to reinvent the wheel and think they know better and can even tell us how we should change our business! If someone is kicking butt and cranking money in their business, it's their prerogative on how to run things. If people are making more money than we are, we'll certainly bounce ideas around and see what we can learn from them. But when someone is making a fraction of our income and think they know better, it boggles our minds.

Becoming an Anti Suit Entrepreneur is ultimately about becoming independent and financially self-sufficient, so you can do what you want. But if you're not there yet, make sure you're not being bull-headed and non-coachable. As with us, most Vested Mentors will stop mentoring people like that.

If you want to "speed up" your journey to becoming an Anti Suit Entrepreneur, then do what Chris did and seek out a Vested Mentor and be coachable.

Don't Mortgage Your House or Life

The most common mistake we see for aspiring entrepreneurs is putting their whole life and assets at risk in their endeavors. You don't have to do this. So many people try their hand at entrepreneurship by purchasing a franchise or similar business that requires an enormous amount of money to start. Not only is a franchise or similar business a risky investment, it really isn't the Anti Suit Entrepreneur lifestyle. Most people who purchase a franchise or similar business end up working harder than they did in their jobs. Additionally, many times these types of businesses require you to use your assets as collateral because many franchises cost $250,000 or more. Most people don't have that type of cash unless they mortgage their house.

Jason started down the Anti Suit Entrepreneur path with spending just over $1,000. Depending on your point of view, that may seem like a lot money or not much at all. From Jason's point of view, it was nothing, because overhead in his family's law firm was over $40,000 a month. When you're looking at starting a business, that $1,000 initial investment is nothing, especially if you compare it to the cost of a franchise. That $1,000 investment was the first step toward Jason becoming an Anti Suit Entrepreneur, earning well over a six-figure Diversified Cash Flow.

Make sure you don't mortgage your life. This is a phrase we coined for not putting yourself into a stupid situation. Over the years, we've seen too many people quit their jobs or live off their savings to pursue the Anti Suit Entrepreneur lifestyle, without having the foundation and infrastructure in place. Be smart; start your Anti Suit Entrepreneur journey part time, while you're working a job to pay the bills. Here's the simple truth; if you can't make money in your business working part time, you're not magically going to make money when you go full time.

Yes, working your business part time will require you to burn the candle at both ends, but it's the smart and safe way to do it. No matter what a potential mentor says to you or how great a business seems, please don't jump into it full time. Trust us. If you spend a few years building up your Anti Suit Business on a part time basis, you'll be much farther ahead. There is nothing wrong with making a good income from your job and from your Anti Suit business, so you can get financially ahead by paying off your mortgage and putting $100,000 in the bank for a rainy day. That's the smart financial move to make and the one we preach to people.

The Five-Year Plan

As stated earlier in our book, it amazes us how most people will spend four to five years (often six to ten years for certain professions) on college in hopes of getting a well-paying job. Yet they won't commit to an entrepreneurship education to enjoy the Anti Suit Entrepreneurship lifestyle. In our society, you are sometimes looked down upon if you are not planning on college.

Attending college for a well-paying job is delayed gratification. Anytime you work for something that provides delayed gratification, and you follow through on it, that process shows a tenacity and focus that some people just don't have. Many people, though, (including the people who have shown that they can work with delayed gratification), exhibit the wrong attitude and behavior when it comes to focusing on a five-year plan for entrepreneurship.

You have to ask if you're ready to commit five years to becoming an Anti Suit Entrepreneur. If a five-year plan sounds as though it's too much time, then entrepreneurship is not for you. You need to have the delayed gratification mindset, if you hope to become an entrepreneur.

Winners Take Action. Losers Make Excuses.

Winners take action, make mistakes, fix those mistakes, and improve. Losers make excuses rather than take action, repeat their mistakes, and never progress. As you're working toward becoming an Anti Suit Entrepreneur ask yourself, "Am I acting like a winner or a loser?" This blunt self-analysis question will help you stay on track. Remember, living life on your terms is a choice. So is choosing to be a winner. If you are ever exhibiting loser type habits, you can change your behavior. In fact, you *will* change it, *if* you choose to.

Basketball fan or not, you probably know who Michael Jordan is. Most people agree that Michael Jordan was the greatest basketball player in history. His work ethic is one of the characteristics that helped him become the greatest. No one had a burning desire to be the best as strongly as Jordan did. He had talent, but so do a lot of people. The difference is that he had an outstanding work habit *and* talent. Talent will help, but you don't need talent in order to become an Anti Suit Entrepreneur. You do need a hard work ethic. Jordan was a winner because he took action and worked harder than anyone else.

In 2004, there was a conference that Chris knew he needed to attend. The conference would provide great networking and information that he knew would help him become an Anti Suit Entrepreneur. The problem was that Chris lived in Blacksburg, Virginia, and the conference was in San Diego, California. If you look up Blacksburg, VA on a map, you'll realize it's not close to very much. Plus, San Diego is an expensive city. The cost for a hotel alone was $300 per night!

There was no way Chris could afford four nights at $300 per night. However, he didn't let that be an excuse and prevent him from going. He figured out how to make his finances work. That solution involved driving four hours to an airport for a cheap flight and staying in a hostel in San Diego for $30 a night. Was there anyone else at the conference staying in a hostel? Nope. But Chris was determined to become an Anti Suit Entrepreneur and had the winner's attitude for making things happen. At first, Chris was embarrassed to tell people at the conference that he was staying at a hostel. Yet, when people found out, he received the opposite reaction than expected from people. It made many people like and admire Chris because they realized he was ambitious and willing to do what was necessary to make things happen. He made some great connections at that event with already successful entrepreneurs because they realized he was hungry for success and willing to work very hard for it.

As you move forward, make sure you maintain the winner's attitude and mindset and figure out how to make things happen.

It's Time to Get Moving!

This is your wake-up call. You can dream about the lifestyle you want, or you can take action toward achieving it. This book has given you powerful insights and valuable guidelines to follow to help you become an Anti Suit Entrepreneur. To get started on your journey, ask yourself, "What do I need to do next?" No book can answer that question for you. But, you probably already know the answer to that question. So take action and start working   toward *living life on your terms.*

CHARGE AHEAD
HOMEWORK

Get it. Read it. **Apply it.**

The "How We Started" video will walk you through the details of our first business. Watch the "How We Started" video at our website www.AntiSuitEntrepreneur.com/chapter12

Made in the USA
Lexington, KY
30 December 2013